Meal Prep

The complete meal prep cookbook for beginners: your essential guide to losing weight and saving time – delicious, simple, and healthy meals to prep and go!

Table of Contents

Introduction **5**

Chapter 1: What Is Meal Prepping? **6**

Chapter 2: Why Meal Prep? 7

Chapter 3: Tips And Tricks **9**

Chapter 4: 9 Rules For Successful Meal Prepping **11**

Chapter 5: How To Meal Prep Like A Pro **14**

Chapter 6: Weight Loss – Nutrition, Calories, Macros and Micros **16**

Chapter 7: Grocery List – Simple, Accessible, And Affordable Ingredients ... **20**

Chapter 8: Meal Prep Recipes **23**

  Breakfast **25**

    Bircher Muesli with Apple and Cinnamon.. 26

    Prepped Tropical Smoothie Freezer Packets 27

    Hard-Boiled Eggs...28

    Prepped Fruit Salad with Lemon and Honey 29

    Berry, Yogurt, and Chia Pots...30

    Salmon and Egg Muffins... 31

    Green smoothie freezer packets..32

    Soaked Oats with Vanilla, Dried Fruit and Nuts.................................... 33

    Toasted Granola Packs (to take to work) 34

    Date and Cocoa Oatmeal Mix..35

    Coconut and Almond Chia Pudding...36

    Avocado, Kale, and Mixed Bean Bowls 37

    Not-So-Hungry Snack Bags 38

    Mango and Lime-Flavored Yogurt 39

    Pre-Made Banana Pancakes..40

    Spinach, Mushroom and Feta Breakfast Pies 41

    Bell Pepper and Bean Burritos...42

    Chorizo and Sweet Potato Hash..43

    Blueberry and mint parfaits..44

    Peanut Butter and Banana Breakfast Cake 45

    Spinach and Zucchini Breakfast Pie with Optional Smoked Fish 46

    Strawberry, Pumpkin Seed and Coconut Oat Baked Crisp 47

    Breakfast Tacos with Eggs, Bell Pepper and Mushrooms........................48

    Salmon, Kale, Ricotta and Egg Fry-pan Cake 50

    Healthy Breakfast Crumble with Stone Fruit and Berries 51

  Lunch **52**

    Quinoa and Fresh Greens Salad..53

    Roasted Veggie Salad 54

    Grilled Chicken with Sweet Potatoes and Asparagus 55

    Brown Rice and Tuna Bowls 56

    Pita Pockets with Lamb and Salad 57

    Sticky Chicken and Broccoli Prep Bowls..58

    Tuna, Corn, and Cheese Hot Sandwiches (for cheat days and cravings)..................59

Stuffed Sweet Potatoes..60
Homemade Hummus, Tomato, and Ham Rice Wafer Stacks 61
Grilled Salmon and Seasonal Greens...62
Chicken, strawberry, and black rice salad..63
Smoked Salmon and Avocado Wholegrain Wraps 64
Cold Tuna and Pasta Salad..65
Cauliflower Rice and Chili Chicken...66
Loaded Broccoli Salad with Toasted Seeds...67
White Bean and Tomato Salad with Balsamic Dressing...........................68
Basil, Tomato and Haloumi Salad with Cos and Cucumber.....................69
Prepped Topping Packs for Rice Wafers..70
Minced Lamb Meat Balls with Yogurt and Cucumber Dip........................71
One-Tray Chicken Thigh and Root Veggie Baked "Bowls".......................72
Cold Soba Noodle Salad with Cashews, Carrot and Tofu 73

Dinner **74**
Freezer Soup (Pumpkin and Coconut)... 75
Spicy Lentil Stew with Sweet Potato Mash and Cilantro 76
Rainbow Chicken Salad..78
Veggie Stacks with Feta and Mint...80
Lamb and Red Onion Skewers..81
Veggie Burgers Patties 82
Mexican-Inspired Shepherd's Pie..83
Swiss Chard and Ricotta Crust-Less Pie 85
Steak and Zoodle Salad...87
Stir-Fried Brown Rice with Chicken and Veggie Jewels..........................88
Prepped Quinoa Sushi Rolls 90
Breaded Fish for the Freezer..92
Green Bean, Potato, and Pea Curry 93
Coconut-Poached Fish with Peanuts and Asian Greens..........................94
Taco Freezer Packets...95
Breaded Chicken Freezer Packets..96
Marinated Steak Freezer Packets...97
Marinated Pork Packets...98
Prepped Pasta Sauce: Tomato...99
Prepped Pasta Sauce: Pesto 100
Prepped Pasta Sauce: Creamy Mushroom 101
Healthy Lamb Curry with Couscous 102
Salmon with Mango and Lentils 104
Freezer Chicken Soup 105

Conclusion..**106**

Introduction

Meal preppers, welcome! This book is *all about* meal prepping, from tips and tricks, benefits and secrets, all the way to recipes for breakfast, lunch, and dinner. If you have a goal to lose weight and trim down, you've started at the right place as meal prepping can really help you to reach your goals. There's something about being organized and dedicated which makes you really want to stick to your goals and eat the foods you know will deliver you to your healthiest weight yet.

These recipes are not "diet" recipes; they are healthy, nutritious, filling, and tasty recipes. I don't believe you need to cut out food groups or deprive yourself in order to lose weight. In fact, eating properly, eating enough, and eating foods that satisfy you will result in weight loss you can maintain and sustain. So, if you're looking for a particular diet or eating style, then this might not be the book for you! But I hope it is, as I know you'll love these recipes as much as I do.

Oh, I should add a bit about me! I am not a nutritionist or dietitian. But I am someone who has successfully lost weight through sensible and healthy eating, and of course, meal prepping! I want to pass on my recipes and my knowledge of meal prepping so you too can experience the same success and health benefits.

Please consult your doctor or nutritionist for advice and guidance if you are looking to lose large amounts of weight, or if you have health issues which might be affected due to a change in diet. This book is a friendly and supportive guideline to help you lose weight in a healthy way, without extreme changes or deprivation.

Now, let's get into the ins and outs of meal prepping!

Chapter 1: What Is Meal Prepping?

Meal prepping is the art of preparing your meals the night (or a few nights) before eating. It usually involves preparing a few portions of each meal, packing them away in airtight containers, and storing in the fridge. Many people prep their meals these days, because it saves time, encourages healthy eating, and controls portions. Sometimes, the meal is completely prepared and cooked in its entirety before being stacked away in the fridge or freezer until it is needed. Whereas sometimes, meals are only partially prepared so they can be cooked right before eating. For example, you can prep lasagna by cooking the sauces and layering it all up before covering and storing in the fridge, raw. You would then place the lasagna into a preheated oven before eating the next night. Whatever prepping method you choose, it's a great way to manage your time and your diet!

Chapter 2: Why Meal Prep?

There are countless reasons to get into the joys of meal prepping, but here are some of the top reasons:

Saves time

By setting aside a chunk of time to get all or most of your meals for the week prepped, you are saving yourself hours of frazzled and rushed cooking throughout the coming days. You can wake up in the morning, grab your prepped breakfast from the fridge, throw your prepped lunch into your bag (ready to eat as soon as you're ready!), and come home to a ready-made dinner you only need to heat in the oven or microwave. Not only do you save *cooking* time, you also save *thinking* time. I don't know about you, but thinking about what to have for breakfast, lunch and dinner always takes up far more of my time than it should!

Saves money

When you decide what to eat for lunch and dinner as you go through the week, you end up heading to the supermarket every couple of days, which increases your chance of spending money on things you don't really need. But when you make a plan of what you will eat for each meal for the entire week, you can do *one* shop where you buy only what you need for those particular meals. You will end up with far less unnecessary items, and more money in your wallet!

Keeps you healthy with portion control and planning

Meal prepping is all about packing away single servings of food for each meal. Therefore, you only make enough for a certain number of portions, with no leftovers. I'm sure you can sympathize with me when I say that leftovers are my absolute downfall! When I don't prep my meals, I end up eating far larger portions than I need, because it's right there in front of me! When you go to eat your breakfast, lunch and dinner, all you have to eat is the single portion you have made, nothing more.

Of course, this does mean you need to prepare sensible portion sizes in the first place, which I have aimed to provide in these recipes. You can adjust the ingredient quantities to suit your personal portion-size preference for your BMI, calorie requirements and activity levels.

Helps you to reach your goals

Quite simply, prepping your meals helps you to remain in control of your eating habits in order to reach your weight loss and health-related goals. You can assess the calories and macros for each recipe and make sure they fit with your weight loss eating plan, so you know that each meal you enjoy is going to help you get to where you want to be.

Gives you some "you time"!

This works two ways! One: the actual meal-prepping process gives you some time for yourself to quietly potter away and enjoy being in the kitchen, with busy hands and lots of creating to do. Two: you will have so much more time to yourself (and for your loved ones) throughout the week when you would usually be rushing around trying to prepare meals from scratch.

Chapter 3: Tips And Tricks

Get a scrap book to keep your favorite recipes and ideas

Trying to think of things to have for each meal can be tiresome and draining, so it's great to have a compilation of your favorite dishes, and some new ones to try too! When you come across a dish you really love and you would like it to be a regular in your rotation, print or write it out and stick it in your homemade recipe book! Hopefully you'll find some new favorites in this book to add to your repertoire.

If you like to freestyle some of your meals and forgo the use of a recipe, make sure you write down the ingredients you used and a rough rundown of the method, so you can recreate it another time! You'll end up with your very own, self-curated recipe book.

Get your partner or family in on the meal-prep fun

If you're prepping for a partner or for your family as well as for yourself, don't take on all the work! Get your family or loved one involved, and treat it as a chance for some quality time for talking and laughing as you prep. If you have kids, give them an easy job so they can practice their food-prep skills while making them feel useful and appreciated in the kitchen with Mom or Dad. This will help to establish meal-prep time as a fun and relaxing thing to do, which means you'll be far more likely to keep the routine up!

Make a dedicated meal-prep box to keep in the pantry

In my pantry, you will find a large box filled with containers, measuring cups and spoons, and a range of regularly-used ingredients. I keep oats, nuts, seeds, canned goods such as beans and corn, olive oil, salt, pepper, herbs, spices, and more. When I embark on each meal-prep session I place this box on the counter and it has all of the essentials I need to create many meals. All I need to do is get my fresh produce, meat and dairy from the fridge and I'm good to go. This makes life quicker and easier as it means you don't need to rummage around in cupboards, shelves, and drawers to find utensils, containers, and ingredients.

Choose a meal-prep day and make sure it's a relaxing experience

If you plan your meal prepping days right, you will begin to really look forward to each meal prep session. It shouldn't be a stressful, rushed, or cumbersome activity, so choose a day when you've got a large chunk of time all to yourself. I find that Sunday afternoons and evenings are the best, as there are rarely social or work activities on Sunday (and there should never be!). I start at 2pm and just meander through the process for as long as it takes and I find it really does relax me. I usually put a podcast or movie on my computer and watch or listen as I quietly work – it's a great time to binge watch a great show! The great thing about Sunday is that you wake up on Monday morning with all of your meals planned and prepped. Choose a day and time that works best for you and do whatever you can to make the experience enjoyable. You could even invite a friend or two around to chatter away with you as you prep (perhaps a nice glass of wine while you're at it?).

Chapter 4: 9 Rules For Successful Meal Prepping

1. *Keep it simple*

Start with simple recipes with minimal ingredients. Most of the recipes in this book are simple and easy to make, without many fancy ingredients or tricky steps. Don't overwhelm yourself by prepping complicated or fiddly dishes – keep it simple until you feel confident to branch out. This will save time and money, and it will make your first prepping experiences easy and enjoyable.

2. *Utilize the freezer*

Frozen prepped meals are a lifesaver during busy and chaotic times. A good way to utilize the freezer is to double the recipe for a particular meal and put half of the servings in the fridge for the consequent days, and put the other half in the freezer for later down the track. You'll be very pleased you did so, especially during times when your meal-prep game schedule is slipping!

3. *Keep your macros in mind: proteins, carbs, fats*

You don't want to sit down to your prepped lunch only to find that it's too filling or not filling enough due to unbalanced macros. Remember to include a portion of protein, some good fats, and some healthy wholegrain carbs for optimum energy and satiety. Most of the recipes in this book have a great balance of macros, but you can adjust them to suit your needs and preferences.

4. *Stock-up on flavor-packing non-perishables*

Herbs, spices, vinegars, oils, and natural flavorings can turn any simple dish into a tasty masterpiece, with very little added calories. What's more, they last a very long time in the pantry so you don't need to worry about using them up before their best-before date. Splash out on a big haul of natural, flavor-giving ingredients to pack into your meal-prep box. This means that you can use simple base ingredients, and adjust the flavors with the addition of healthy and low-cal seasonings.

5. *Invest in storage equipment*

This is an important one. To successfully prep, you need containers to store your meals in. High-quality plastic or glass containers with airtight lids are ideal, especially if you can find a set which includes different sizes. Small, single-serve containers are really handy for breakfasts such as oats and chia pudding, and snacks such as fruit and nut mix. Pyrex bowls which have airtight lids are ideal for large salads and soups. Have a shop around and find yourself a few value packs, and allocate a special box, drawer, or cupboard, especially for your meal-prep containers.

6. Get creative with color

During my own meal prepping journey I found that using bright and varied colors really helped me to get excited about making, and eating my prepped meals. A pile of red cabbage with bright red bell peppers and some vibrant green cilantro – beautiful! Rich yellow corn kernels, inky black beans, glossy red chili, and pale green avocado, it looks as amazing as it tastes. If you're like me, then you'll get a kick out of putting together beautiful and fresh-looking meals to fill your containers. Fresh fruits, veggies, herbs, and rich spices are the best sources of edible color.

7. Predict your cravings and prep accordingly

If you don't feel like eating a particular meal, then don't prep it. Don't think that you must eat a certain type of dish simply because it seems like the healthiest option. You can make any dish healthy! Even if it's traditionally a junk food. For example, you will find recipes for burgers and rich pastas in this book, but they are nutritious versions which fit in with your weight loss plans. If you've got a craving for sweeter dishes, then try a yummy oatmeal with dates for breakfast! If you feel like something a bit heavier for dinner (tiredness, hormones, and overindulgence can make us crave comfort foods) then choose a recipe for dinner with sweet potatoes and beans to fill you up. The bottom line? Prep foods you want to eat that particular week! This way, you'll avoid seeking other foods or snacks to satisfy you in between meals.

8. Make a plan and stick to it

This is where you need to be a bit strict and structured. Decide on a day to complete your prepping, set the time aside, and stick to it. Get your shopping done on the same day so your produce and meats are fresh, then set aside a couple of hours to prep, prep, prep! If you end up missing a prep day and you don't have the time to make up for it, you might find you slip back into day-to-day meals and the unhealthy choices and unbalanced portion sizes may creep back. Once the routine has been established it will be so easy!

9. *Make it fun*

Cooking should be as fun as eating, in my opinion! And the same goes for prepping. If you enjoy yourself, you'll get into a positive mindset about meal prepping, and a positive mindset about food will follow on. There are many ways to make meal-prep sessions fun! Play music, have a glass of wine, watch your favorite TV show, anything that relaxes you and puts you at ease as you work. Weight loss needn't be a drag, it can actually be an enjoyable and nourishing experience if you make the process work in a way that you enjoy.

Chapter 5: How To Meal Prep Like A Pro

You will get into your own meal-prep rhythm, but here is a step-by-step guide to meal prepping like a pro which you can use to guide you when you first get started.

Schedule your prep day

Take a look at your diary or calendar (or app on your phone you use to schedule your days!) and find a day when you can set aside a good 3 hours for prepping. Weekends are ideal, especially Sundays, so you can prep for the entire week coming. Set time aside for meal planning, shopping, and prepping. Don't double-book yourself, treat it like an important appointment you must keep.

Write your meal plan

Sit down with a pad and paper and write down what you want to eat for breakfast, lunch, and dinner for the week ahead. Try to keep it to 2 variations per week. For example: 2 different options for breakfast, lunch and dinner, as opposed to a different meal every day, or the same thing every day.

Write out a shopping list based on your meal plan, taking into account the items you already have in your kitchen.

Go shopping

Head to the supermarket and strictly follow your shopping list! Don't be tempted to stray and buy items you don't need. When you get home, unpack your groceries and place them in easy-to-find places, or even leave them on the bench if you're going to prep immediately. Remember to refrigerate meats and dairy. If you have a "prep box", put your dried or nonperishable goods into it so they're ready to go for prepping.

Prep

First, figure out which steps you can multi-task. If you need to cook something in the oven, prepare to get another task done as it cooks. If you need to let something soak or cool, use that time to complete other steps. Figure out which meals are the most time-consuming and get started on those first, using little bits of spare time in the process to complete quicker tasks such as mixing granola or slicing fresh veggies.

Pack, label and store

Before you begin, it's a good idea to clear a shelf in your fridge (and freezer, if using) so you don't have to shuffle things around and pack things into awkward places when it comes time to store.

Use the most compact container you can when it's time to store your meals. This is when having a range of different sizes will come in very handy!

If you like, you can label your containers by sticking a removable, plain sticker onto the lid and marking it with a marker. Write down the date you cooked/prepped the meal so you know how long it has been in the fridge. This will help you to ensure your meals are always fresh.

Pack away your prepped meals, clean up, sit back, and relax!

Chapter 6: Weight Loss – Nutrition, Calories, Macros and Micros

How weight loss works – with a personal story to match!

This will have to be a simplified version of the weight loss process! And keep in mind, not everyone is the same and some people lose weight more easily than others, and others may keep weight on for various health reasons. Make sure you see your doctor first if you are aiming to lose weight, as they can look through your medical history and point out any potential patterns or issues, which could help you to find the best method for you. Now that that's out of the way, we can get into the general rules and sciences behind weight loss.

So, when you eat food, you are taking in energy (calories). When you move and exercise, you are burning calories. When you burn more calories than what you are eating, you will lose weight. Keep in mind that your body needs a basic number of calories in order to survive and keep your organs running, which is why it's very important to eat enough. I add this because when I first started to consider calories I was a bit taken aback by the notion of "burning more calories than you take in", thinking I would have to burn 1800 calories worth of exercise a day! But perhaps that was just my very silly mistake; you are probably a lot more intelligent than that!

When you reach a calorie deficit, your body begins to turn to energy sources, which are already in your body, i.e. stored fat. Sometimes, muscle can also be used for energy, which does result in weight loss, but it also results in muscle loss and a less-toned physique. You can remedy this by incorporating strength training into your fitness routine, as well as high intensity cardio. By doing this, you are helping your body to burn fat as well as building muscle at the same time. You also need to eat properly to give your body enough protein and energy to get through those workouts and repair those muscles properly afterward!

Some people opt for the low-calorie method of weight loss, and I have also done that. It worked for a while but I couldn't sustain it, so I had to turn to another method. I decided to ramp-up my workouts and eat a more well-rounded diet, full of nutritious foods, and enough of them. By training with weights and high intensity cardio, my metabolism became faster and more efficient, and my increased muscle mass helped me to burn more calories.

Calories

"Calories" is basically another word for energy. When you eat, you are consuming energy, which your body uses to function and grow. If you eat too many calories, you will put on weight, if you reduce them, you will lose weight. You can figure out how many calories you need in order to lose weight by punching your weight, height, age, gender and activity level into an online calorie-counter. It will tell you how many calories you need to eat in order to lose, gain or maintain weight. A good rule of thumb is to reduce your calorific intake by 300-500. This can be done pretty easily just by cutting out high-calorie foods such as processed treats, cakes, ice cream, white starches and alcohol.

Macronutrients

Macronutrients are the main groups your food is categorized under: carbs, fats, and proteins. Each of these has a particular function in the body, and they are all important for weight loss and general health. I know there are many people out there who banish carbs, but let's make this book a carb-friendly zone!

Carbohydrates

Carbs give you energy! Your body adores carbs because it's an easy energy source. Carbohydrates, especially those found in starchy or sugary foods are often very high in calories, which is why people avoid overeating carbs when trying to manage their weight. When you don't burn off the energy you consume, your body stores it as fat – so it's best to eat a high-carb meal on days when you are active and exercising. As long as you eat carbs which come from whole, natural sources with slow-releasing energy, there's absolutely no need to fear them! If you want to eat bread? Opt for a wholegrain sourdough from a real bakery as opposed to a white loaf from the supermarket (these are often full of sugar and refined white flour). If you feel like pasta? Opt for a whole-meal variety and take note of the serving size on the packet and stick to it so you don't add extra calories with large portions.

Carbs to eat:

- Starchy veggies such as sweet potatoes
- Fruits and berries
- Whole grains such as quinoa, brown rice, oats
- Wholegrain breads and pastas

Carbs to avoid:

- Processed, white flour (cakes and baked goods, white bread)
- White pasta
- White rice (in moderation is fine, but brown rice is far better)
- Sugary foods (sweets, cakes, ice cream...all of the classic sugary snacks!)

Fat

Healthy fats are important for the body to function properly. Fats make you feel satiated and full, and they help the body to absorb and process essential nutrients and proteins. Good fats found in foods such as fish and avocadoes are great for cognitive (brain) health and keeping the skin in good condition. Adding a source of healthy fat to your dinner will help you to feel satisfied. Opt for nuts, seeds, avocado, fish and olive oil.

Fatty foods to eat:

- Avocadoes
- Nuts and seeds
- Olive oil
- Oily fish such as salmon and tuna

Fatty foods to avoid:

- Fried foods (fast foods)
- Processed fats such as margarine

Protein

Protein is very important for muscle growth, that's why hard-core lifters are always guzzling protein shakes and egg whites! If we didn't eat any protein, our cells, bones, muscles, nails, (basically our whole body!) couldn't repair and renew itself and grow stronger. It's important to incorporate protein into your diet so your body can remain strong and supported. Protein is also very satiating so it fills you up and keeps cravings at bay.

Protein to eat:

- Eggs
- Lean red meat
- Lean chicken
- Fish
- Unsweetened yogurt
- Beans and lentils
- Tofu

Protein to avoid:

- Fatty meats

Micronutrients

Micronutrients are far more commonly known as vitamins and minerals. We usually take supplements and pills to boost our micronutrients, especially in the winter when we are prone to get sick. However, you really can get enough micronutrients through a proper diet (unless you have a condition which hinders your body's ability to absorb and hold onto certain micronutrients). As long as you eat lots of fresh fruits, veggies, lean meats, grains and seeds you should be getting enough micronutrients. However, blood tests can detect micronutrient deficiencies and you can take supplements to remedy this.

Important micronutrients to keep an eye out for:

- Iron
- Magnesium
- Folate
- Calcium
- Zinc
- B, A, C and E vitamins

Chapter 7: Grocery List – Simple, Accessible, And Affordable Ingredients

This grocery list is a rough guide to healthy shopping and these ingredients are all featured in the recipes for breakfast, lunch and dinner. Please feel free to adjust the list according to what's in season, especially when it comes to fresh produce.

I haven't added quantities for you, because you may be feeding one person, or you may be feeding many! So simply plan your meals for the week, figure out how many portions you will be making, and choose your quantities accordingly.

Happy shopping!

Fresh produce:
- Carrots
- Broccoli
- Spinach
- Kale
- Onions
- Garlic
- Bananas
- Zucchini
- Swiss chard
- Bell peppers (all colors)
- Green onions (scallions)

Frozen goods:
- Frozen mixed berries
- Frozen green beans

Dairy and eggs:
- Free range eggs
- Whole milk
- Feta cheese
- Ricotta cheese
- Cheddar cheese

Meat and fish:
- Chicken thighs
- Chicken breasts
- Lean beef steak
- Lean lamb leg steak
- Smoked salmon
- Fresh white fish fillets

Breads and pastas:
- Wholegrain pasta
- Wholegrain or sourdough bread
- Wholegrain wraps
- Wholegrain pita breads

Grains:
- Quinoa
- Wholegrain rolled oats
- Brown rice
- Couscous

Nuts, seeds and dried fruits:
- Whole raw almonds
- Whole raw walnuts
- Pumpkin seeds
- Sunflower seeds
- Chia seeds
- Flaxseeds
- Dates
- Prunes
- Raisins
- Dried apricots
- Desiccated or threaded coconut
- Nori sheets (seaweed)

Oils, sauces vinegars:

- Olive oil
- Coconut oil
- Apple cider vinegar
- Balsamic vinegar
- Sesame oil
- Soy sauce
- Lamb broth
- Chicken broth
- Beef broth

Canned goods:

- Black beans
- Kidney beans
- Corn kernels
- Canned chopped tomatoes
- Coconut milk
- Canned lentils

Chapter 8: Meal Prep Recipes

About these recipes

You will have noticed when reading the shopping list, these recipes do not cut out any food groups. I don't believe you must cut carbs or fat in order to lose weight! As long as you are active and you are eating fresh, whole food and being mindful of portion sizes, you can eat the foods you love. One thing these recipes do *not* contain is refined sugar. Fruit, and the odd drizzle of honey may make an appearance, but none of the processed stuff!

Serves

Each recipe states how many servings it makes. If you are prepping your meals only for yourself, then you will have as many servings as the recipe makes. But if you are cooking for two, then you will have half, and your partner will have half. Therefore, keep in mind how many days you want a particular recipe to last for, and adjust the quantities accordingly. For example, if you want Bircher muesli every day for 6 days for yourself, then make one and a half times the recipe to make 6 servings (the recipe makes 4). I haven't made each recipe cater to a whole week because not all recipes are great after a few days in the fridge, but that's up to you!

Containers

Containers are KEY when it comes to meal prepping. I have indicated which kind of containers you will need to store each prepped recipe. Most of them are pretty flexible and a normal bowl covered with cling wrap is completely fine. However, if you're planning on taking your prepped meals (especially lunches) to work, then airtight containers with reliable lids are the best. Look for some bargains and get a few value packs of containers!

Time

This simply refers to the amount of time it will take you to complete the prepped meal, including any cooking if required. It does not include overnight chilling time. These times are approximate, as everyone preps at a different pace!

Ingredients

Just as it sounds, this is where you find all of the ingredients you will need to make your prepped meal. I haven't added salt or pepper to the ingredients lists as I'm certain you will have those ingredients at the ready at all times.

Directions

I have aimed to provide clear and precise directions so you can get your meal prepping done quickly, without having to guess or decipher missing steps.

Nutritional content

Here you will find the approximate calorie count, and the fat, protein and carbohydrate content in grams for each *serving*. I have used My Fitness Pal to gather this information, which is a very accurate source. However, I might use different brands of certain foods which might alter the nutritional content slightly, so please take these numbers as approximate and not exact.

Breakfast

I believe in eating a filling, energy-rich breakfast every day, especially when trying to lose weight. Many of these recipes contain wholegrain rolled oats, which I consider to be a Holy Grail ingredient! The carbohydrate content in of most of these recipes is pretty high, because I think it's best to consume the majority of your carbs in the first half of the day for energy. There is a mixture of sweet and savory, hot and cold recipes to choose from.

Bircher Muesli with Apple and Cinnamon

Oats and grated apple, soaked in yoghurt and milk overnight, with a hint of warming cinnamon. This is a very simplified recipe, as I find that a less "busy" bircher in the morning is best. However, you can add extra nuts and seeds if you wish, just remember that it will change the nutritional information.

Serves: 4 prepped servings
Container: 4 small containers or small bowls or ramekins
Time: approximately 10 minutes

Nutritional info per serving:
- Calories: 185
- Fat: 3 grams
- Protein: 4 grams
- Carbs: 33 grams

Ingredients:
- 1 ½ cups wholegrain rolled oats
- 2 apples, skin on, grated
- 1 tsp. ground cinnamon
- 1 cup almond milk (or any other milk you prefer)
- 1 cup plain, unsweetened yogurt

Method:
1. Place the oats, grated apple, cinnamon, milk, and yogurt into a bowl and stir to combine. The mixture should be wet and reasonably thick, but it will depend on the brand of yogurt you use. If your mixture seems a bit too dry or too thick, add a bit more milk, or even some water if you don't want to change the calorie count.
2. Divide the mixture into your four containers or bowls, cover, and place in the fridge.
3. In the morning, simply grab it from the fridge and eat with a spoon! You'll love this cold, filling, and refreshing breakfast.

Prepped Tropical Smoothie Freezer Packets

Smoothie freezer packets are lifesavers! These ones are full of tropical ingredients for a fresh and naturally sweet morning smoothie. Simply add water or milk, blitz, and drink. Easy! Note: adding milk will adjust the nutritional info as the info provided is for the contents of the smoothie packet only.

Serves: 7 freezer packets (one smoothie per packet)
Container: 7 small sealable, freezer-friendly bags
Time: approximately 10 minutes

Nutritional info per serving – with water added only:
- Calories: 145
- Fat: 1 gram
- Protein: 3 grams
- Carbs: 36 grams

Ingredients:
- 3 bananas, peeled and chopped into chunks
- 2 fresh mangoes, peeled, flesh cut into chunks
- 3 cups frozen or fresh mixed berries
- 2 cups chopped kale

Method:
1. Place the banana, mango, berries, and kale into a bowl and stir to combine.
2. Divide the mixture into your 7 freezer-safe bags, seal, and place in the freezer.
3. In the morning, simply throw the contents of one freezer smoothie packet into your blender, add a cup of water or milk (coconut milk would be great with this recipe!) and blend. For some extra sustenance, you could add a handful of oats and some yogurt.

Hard-Boiled Eggs

As boring as this "recipe" may sound, boiled eggs are a meal-preppers dream. A boiled egg is a great "side dish" to any breakfast, as they provide a great dose of protein. A boiled egg and a prepped smoothie for breakfast? Yes please.

Serves: 7 boiled eggs (one egg per serving, as a protein hit)
Container: you can store these any way you like, you could even put them in the egg holder inside your fridge to save using a separate bowl or container
Time: approximately 20 minutes (including cooling time)

Nutritional info per serving:
- Calories: 70
- Fat: 5 grams
- Protein: 6 grams
- Carbs: 0 grams

Ingredients:
- 7 eggs

Method:
1. Bring a pot of water to the boil (enough water to thoroughly cover the eggs).
2. Bring the temperature down slightly so the boiling is not so vigorous.
3. Very gently place the eggs into the pot with a large spoon.
4. Set the timer for 9 minutes and leave the eggs to gently boil.
5. Once the timer beeps, place the pot under a tap of cold water until all of the water in the pot is cold.
6. Leave the eggs to cool in the cold water for about 10 minutes before placing them in the fridge.
7. I leave the shell of my hard-boiled eggs until right before eating them, as I find it easier to store them with shell on.

Prepped Fruit Salad with Lemon and Honey

Look, I know many people would say that eating lots of fruit (and added honey!) is not "healthy" for weight loss due to the sugar content. However, these are natural sugars, and these fruits also provide lots of fiber and awesome vitamins. What's more, I find that if I have fresh fruit in the morning it seems to stop any sugar cravings from creeping in throughout the day.

Serves: 3 (should be eaten within 3 days for maximum freshness)
Container: 3 sealable containers
Time: approximately 10 minutes

Nutritional info per serving:
- Calories: 176
- Fat: 0 grams
- Protein: 2 grams
- Carbs: 46 grams

Ingredients:
- 2 bananas, cut into chunks
- 4 large strawberries, cut into quarters
- 1 apple, core removed, flesh cut into small chunks
- 1 orange, cut into chunks
- 2 tbsp. honey
- 1 juicy lemon

Method:
1. Place the bananas, strawberries, apple, orange, honey, and juice of one lemon in a bowl and stir to combine.
2. Divide the fruit salad into your 3 containers, cover, and store in the fridge.
3. For extra protein, serve with plain Greek yogurt or a hard-boiled egg on the side.

Berry, Yogurt, and Chia Pots

Chia seeds are full of fiber, protein, and fatty acids, which make them a filling and energy-giving breakfast ingredient. These pots are cooling, tangy, and slightly sweet thanks to the berry surprise at the bottom.

Serves: 5 pots (1 pot per serving)
Container: 5 glass pots with lids, or cups with cling wrap to cover
Time: approximately 10 minutes

Nutritional info per serving:
- Calories: 139
- Fat: 5 grams
- Protein: 4 grams
- Carbs: 17 grams

Ingredients:
- 2 cups mixed berries (frozen or fresh, I use frozen raspberries and blueberries)
- 6 tbsp. chia seeds
- 1 cup (8floz) almond milk
- ½ cup (4floz) cold water
- 1 tsp. cinnamon
- 1 tsp. vanilla extract
- 1 cup (8floz) plain, unsweetened yogurt

Method:
1. Divide the berries between your 5 pots or cups.
2. Place the chia seeds, almond milk, water, cinnamon, and vanilla extract into a small bowl and stir to combine.
3. Divide the chia seed mixture between the 5 pots, and spoon on top of the berries.
4. Divide the yogurt between the 5 pots and spoon on top of the chia mixture.
5. Sprinkle a little bit of cinnamon on top of the yogurt and place an extra berry on top (mostly for looks, but a pretty breakfast is an enjoyable one!).
6. Cover and place into the fridge.

Salmon and Egg Muffins

A small amount of smoked salmon goes a long way. The fat content and rich saltiness is very satiating, while the eggs are filling without loading-up on carbs. These are great for when you just want a small breakfast.

Serves: 6 muffins (1 muffin per serving)
Container: keep muffins in an airtight container in the fridge
Time: approximately 15 minutes

Nutritional info per serving:
- Calories: 93
- Fat: 6 grams
- Protein: 8 grams
- Carbs: 1 gram

Ingredients:
- 4 eggs
- 1/3 cup milk
- Salt and pepper, to taste
- 1 ½ oz. smoked salmon, cut into small pieces
- 1 tbsp. finely chopped chives

Method:
1. Preheat the oven to 356 degrees Fahrenheit and grease 6 muffin tin holes with a small amount of butter.
2. Place the eggs, milk, and a pinch of salt and pepper into a small bowl and lightly beat to combine.
3. Divide the egg mixture between the 6 muffin holes, then divide the salmon between the muffins and place into each hole, gently pressing down to submerge in the egg mixture.
4. Sprinkle each muffin with chopped chives and place in the oven for about 8-10 minutes or until just set.
5. Leave to cool for about 5 minutes before turning out and storing in an airtight container in the fridge.

Green smoothie freezer packets

Getting your greens in the morning always feels good, like you're checking something important off the list before you even leave the house! The blueberries might make this smoothie a little less green and more purple... but I still call it a green smoothie because of the spinach, kale, and green apples!

Serves: 7 freezer packets (one smoothie per packet)
Container: 7 small sealable, freezer-friendly bags
Time: approximately 10 minutes

Nutritional info per serving – with water added only:

- Calories: 105
- Fat: 3 grams
- Protein: 2 grams
- Carbs: 18 grams

Ingredients:

- 4 cups baby spinach leaves
- 2 cups chopped raw kale
- 1 avocado, flesh cut into chunks
- 2 green apples, skin on, cut into chunks
- 2 cups blueberries

Method:

1. Place the spinach, kale, avocado, apples, and blueberries into a bowl and stir to combine.
2. Divide the smoothie mixture between the 7 bags, seal, and place into the freezer.
3. To make the smoothie, place the contents of one smoothie packet into the blender, and add enough water to suit your preferred smoothie consistency.
4. You could also use almond milk, coconut water, or yogurt, but keep in mind it will alter the nutritional information.

Soaked Oats with Vanilla, Dried Fruit and Nuts

This is a recipe for very busy, active days, as the carb-count is generous and the energy rating is high! A great breakfast for after a morning run or gym session. Add some Greek yoghurt for extra protein, but remember it will change the nutritional info.

Serves: 4 soaked-oat pots
Container: 4 jars with lids, or 4 cups or ramekins with cling wrap to cover
Time: approximately 10 minutes

Nutritional info per serving:
- Calories: 300
- Fat: 11 grams
- Protein: 9 grams
- Carbs: 41 grams

Ingredients:
- 2 cups whole grain rolled oats
- 3 cups (24floz) almond milk
- 3 tsp. vanilla extract
- 4 prunes, chopped into small pieces
- 4 dates, chopped into small pieces
- 20 almonds, roughly chopped
- 12 walnuts, roughly chopped

Method:
1. Place the oats, almond milk, vanilla extract, prunes, dates, almonds, and walnuts into a bowl and stir to combine.
2. Divide the mixture into the 4 jars, seal or cover, then place into the fridge to soak overnight.
3. In the morning, if you find that the oats are a bit too stiff or dry for your liking, you can add a bit more almond milk to loosen it up.

Toasted Granola Packs (to take to work)

On mornings when you have no time to eat breakfast at home, or you're not quite ready to eat yet, a portable pack of granola is the handiest option. Throw it in your bag and use the milk at your work (or take a little bottle of milk with you). And I'll admit, sometimes I like to snack on this granola dry, almost like a trail mix! Seeds provide healthy fats, and oats provide slow-release energy.

Serves: 7 packs (1 serving per pack)
Container: 7 small airtight containers or sealable bags
Time: approximately 15 minutes

Nutritional info per serving:
- Calories: 261
- Fat: 11 grams
- Protein: 12 grams
- Carbs: 33 grams

Ingredients:
- 2 tbsp. coconut oil
- 3 cups wholegrain rolled oats
- 4 tbsp. shredded coconut
- 3 tbsp. flaxseeds
- 3 tbsp. pumpkin seeds
- 3 tbsp. sunflower seeds
- 3 tbsp. chia seeds
- 10 dried apricots, chopped into small pieces
- 1 tsp. cinnamon
- ¼ tsp. sea salt

Method:
1. Heat the coconut oil in a large pan or pot over a medium heat.
2. Add the oats, coconut, flaxseeds, pumpkin seeds, sunflower seeds, chia seeds, dried apricots, cinnamon, and sea salt, stir to combine.
3. Keep stirring the mixture as it gently toasts for about 7 minutes or until golden and aromatic (it will smell like fresh baking!).
4. Leave in the pan to cool before filling your 7 bags or containers.
5. Store in the pantry.

Date and Cocoa Oatmeal Mix

The reason for the inclusion of cocoa is pretty obvious...chocolate! Without the sugar and calories, of course. The dates provide a caramel-like sweetness to this amazing oatmeal, but if you're not a fan of oats, use any other dried fruit you like. The nutritional information provided here is only for the contents of the dry oatmeal mix, so you will have to add whichever milk you use to the calories and macros.

Serves: 7 servings of oatmeal
Container: you can either store this in one large container, or divide it into 7 single-serve containers
Time: approximately 10 minutes

Nutritional info per serving:
- Calories: 191
- Fat: 2 grams
- Protein: 7 grams
- Carbs: 37 grams

Ingredients:
- 4 cups wholegrain rolled oats
- 1 tbsp. unsweetened cocoa powder
- 15 dates, chopped into small pieces
- Pinch of salt

Method:
1. Place the oats, cocoa, dates, and salt into a bowl and stir to combine.
2. Place into one large container or 7 small containers and store in the pantry.
3. To make the oatmeal, place one serving of dry mix into a pot and add 1 and ¼ cups (10fl oz.) of water or milk, stir, and simmer until thick.

Coconut and Almond Chia Pudding

More chia seeds! I can't get enough of them. They're so filling and full of fiber (which is a major essential for weight loss). This recipe uses almond essence, chopped almonds, and coconut milk. It's a great recipe to choose when you feel like something a bit sweet and creamy.

Serves: 4 puddings
Container: 4 jars or small bowls with cling film to cover, or 4 containers with lids
Time: approximately 10 minutes (plus chilling overnight)

Nutritional info per serving:
- Calories: 296
- Fat: 19 grams
- Protein: 10 grams
- Carbs: 24 grams

Ingredients:
- 6 tbsp. chia seeds
- 1 cup wholegrain rolled oats
- 4 tbsp. desiccated coconut
- ½ tsp. almond essence
- ½ tsp. vanilla extract
- 4 cups (32fl oz.) unsweetened coconut milk
- 32 raw almonds, roughly chopped

Method:
1. Place the chia seeds, oats, desiccated coconut, almond essence, vanilla extract, coconut milk, and raw almonds into a bowl and stir to combine.
2. Divide between your 4 jars or containers, cover, and place in the fridge overnight.
3. The chia seeds will expand and become gelatinous as they absorb moisture, so give the pudding a good stir before eating.

Avocado, Kale, and Mixed Bean Bowls

Now a recipe for lovers of savory breakfasts! Beans, avocado and kale are a super trio of fats, fiber, and good carbs. You can serve these bowls hot or cold, and they can even be eaten for lunch. If you need an extra dose of protein (perhaps after a session of heavy lifting) add a poached egg on top!

Serves: 4 bowls (1 serving per bowl)
Container: 4 airtight containers
Time: approximately 20 minutes

Nutritional info per serving:
- Calories: 290
- Fat: 11 grams
- Protein: 12 grams
- Carbs: 38 grams

Ingredients:
- ½ onion, finely chopped
- ½ tsp paprika
- 1 fresh tomato, chopped into chunks
- 1 can (14 oz.) black beans, drained
- 1 can (14 oz.) kidney beans, drained
- Salt and pepper, to taste
- 2 avocadoes, flesh sliced
- 2 cups chopped kale (chop it quite finely as kale tends to be tough)

Method:
1. Drizzle a small amount of olive oil into a pot and place over a low heat, add the onions, paprika, tomato, black beans, and kidney beans and stir to combine.
2. Simmer over a medium heat for about 10 minutes until bubbling and thick, and add a pinch of salt and pepper to season.
3. Divide the bean mixture between your 4 bowls and leave to cool slightly before placing the sliced avocado and kale on top.
4. Drizzle some extra olive oil over top of the kale and avocado before covering with plastic wrap and placing into the fridge until needed.

Not-So-Hungry Snack Bags

You know those mornings when you just can't stomach a full-on breakfast, and you just want a little something to nibble on? That's what this recipe is for. No cooking involved here, just gathering a few simple dry ingredients and packing them into little bags or containers. Even though these snack bags are small, they provide a good dose of energy and healthy fat.

Serves: 7 snack bags (1 serving per snack bag)
Container: 7 sealable bags or airtight containers (small ones will do)
Time: approximately 10 minutes

Nutritional info per serving:
- Calories: 276
- Fat: 18 grams
- Protein: 10 grams
- Carbs: 24 grams

Ingredients:
- 14 prunes
- 14 dried apricots
- 14 whole walnuts
- ½ cup raw almonds
- 14 macadamia nuts
- ¼ cup pumpkin seeds

Method:
1. Divide each ingredient into your 7 containers or bags, seal, and place in the pantry. Very easy!
2. If you like, you could make the pieces smaller by chopping the dates, prunes, and nuts into small pieces, almost like trail mix.
3. Keep these bags in your handbag or office desk for a healthy snack when cravings hit.

Mango and Lime-Flavored Yogurt

Fresh, cold, creamy Greek yoghurt is one of my favorite things to eat for breakfast, especially when I know I need some extra probiotics and some protein to help my muscles repair from a lifting session. While the pre-flavored yoghurt varieties are often full of refined sugar, this version is flavored by you, at home, with ingredients you can trust. Mangoes, honey, and lime...you could even eat it as a dessert treat!

Serves: 5 servings
Container: 5 small airtight containers
Time: approximately 10 minutes

Nutritional info per serving:
- Calories: 266
- Fat: 14 grams
- Protein: 7 grams
- Carbs: 30 grams

Ingredients:
- 2 mangoes, flesh removed and cut into small pieces
- 3 cups (24fl oz.) unsweetened Greek yogurt
- 1 tbsp. honey
- 1 lime

Method:
1. Place half of the mango into a blender, or use a stick blender, and blend to a pulp.
2. Place the blended mango, remaining mango chunks, yogurt, honey, and grated zest of one lime into a bowl and stir to combine.
3. Divide into your 5 containers, cover, and store in the fridge.
4. For an extra treat, sprinkle a few chopped almonds or some desiccated coconut on top before eating.

Pre-Made Banana Pancakes

These pancakes do not contain any sugar, flour or butter! Bananas, eggs and ground almonds are the main ingredients. Bananas provide potassium and sweetness, eggs add the protein, and ground almonds contain healthy fats. Fry them up during your prep session, store them in the fridge, then zap them in the microwave or frying pan to heat before serving.

Serves: 15 pancakes (5 servings, 3 pancakes per serving)
Container: 1 airtight container to store all of the pancakes is ideal
Time: approximately 25 minutes

Nutritional info per serving:
- Calories: 170
- Fat: 11 grams
- Protein: 6 grams
- Carbs: 14 grams

Ingredients:
- 2 large bananas, peeled and cut into chunks
- 3 eggs
- ½ cup ground almonds
- 1 tsp. vanilla extract
- ½ tsp baking powder
- Coconut oil, for frying

Method:
1. Place the bananas, eggs, ground almonds, vanilla extract, and baking powder into a bowl and mash using a fork, handheld stick blender, or potato masher until smooth and combined.
2. Drizzle some coconut oil into a non-stick frying pan and place over a medium heat until oil gets hot.
3. Place scoop of pancake mixture into the hot pan and cook on both sides until golden and cooked through.
4. Place the cooked pancakes into your airtight container and store in the fridge.
5. Before eating the next morning, simply heat the pancakes in the microwave or on a dry, hot frying pan until heated through.
6. Serve with yogurt and fruit, or simply eat plain!

Spinach, Mushroom and Feta Breakfast Pies

These pies are SO light in calories, you can have them as a snack on the side of a more robust breakfast. They are a great way to get extra protein and a dose of greens in the morning. The feta cheese adds creaminess and a tart saltiness to satisfy your taste buds.

Serves: 1 large pie to be cut into 8 pieces (8 servings)
Container: store in the fridge in a large airtight container with baking paper to separate the layers of pie slices so they don't stick together
Time: approximately 25 minutes

Nutritional info per serving:
- Calories: 67
- Fat: 5 grams
- Protein: 5 grams
- Carbs: 1 gram

Ingredients:
- 5 eggs
- 2 cups chopped spinach
- 1 cup sliced mushrooms (any kind)
- 2 oz. feta cheese, cut into small pieces, or crumbled
- Salt and pepper, to taste

Method:
1. Preheat the oven to 356 degrees Fahrenheit and grease a rectangular pie or casserole dish with butter.
2. Place the eggs, spinach, mushrooms, feta, salt, and pepper into a bowl and whisk to combine.
3. Pour the mixture into the greased dish and place into the oven to bake for about 10 minutes until just set.
4. Leave to cool before slicing into 8 pieces and placing into an airtight container.
5. Store in the fridge.

Bell Pepper and Bean Burritos

These burritos are ideal for power days when you've got lots of exercise, work, and running around to do. Packed with fiber and protein from beans and eggs, and the sweetness of softened bell peppers. Fresh cilantro and red chili offer a hit of fresh flavor and bright color.

Serves: 4 burritos (1 burrito is 1 serving)
Container: 4 single-serve airtight containers, or 1 large one to store all 4 burritos
Time: approximately 20 minutes

Nutritional info per serving:
- Calories: 310
- Fat: 8 grams
- Protein: 14 grams
- Carbs: 45 grams

Ingredients:
- 2 garlic cloves, finely chopped
- 2 red bell peppers, finely sliced
- 1 tsp. paprika
- ½ tsp. chili powder
- 1 can (14 oz.) black beans, drained
- Salt and pepper, to taste
- 2 eggs, lightly beaten
- 4 small flour or corn tortillas
- Fresh cilantro, chopped
- ½ fresh red chili, finely chopped

Method:
1. Drizzle some olive oil into a frying pan and place over a medium heat.
2. Add the garlic, bell peppers, paprika, and chili powder, sauté until the bell peppers are soft.
3. Add the black beans and a pinch of salt and pepper, stir to combine, continue to sauté.
4. Push the bean and bell pepper mixture to one side of the pan and pour the lightly beaten eggs on the other side, stir them as they scramble until just cooked.
5. Turn off the heat and lay your tortillas onto a board.
6. Fill each tortilla with bell pepper, beans, and eggs.
7. Sprinkle with cilantro and fresh chili, and tightly wrap.
8. Carefully place the burritos into your container/s, cover, and place into the fridge.

Chorizo and Sweet Potato Hash

Okay, you got me... chorizo isn't a "weight loss" food, but it's tasty, salty, and full of flavor to satisfy you throughout the morning. A little bit of chorizo sausage is not going to sabotage your weight-loss goals, so go ahead and enjoy it! Sweet potato provides fiber and good carbs, and eggs provide that ever-important protein. Slice this hash into 4 pieces, store them away in the fridge, and eat hot or cold for a tasty, savory breakfast.

Serves: 4
Container: 1 large airtight container to store all 4 pieces, or 4 single-serve containers
Time: approximately 25 minutes

Nutritional info per serving:
- Calories: 236
- Fat: 11 grams
- Protein: 12 grams
- Carbs: 24 grams

Ingredients:
- 3 cups sweet potato, cubed (about 2 large sweet potatoes)
- 1 chorizo sausage, sliced
- 1 cup spinach leaves, chopped
- 3 eggs, lightly beaten

Method:
1. Place the sweet potatoes into a pot and cover with water, place over a medium heat until boiling. Leave to simmer, uncovered, until the sweet potatoes are soft but not mushy.
2. Drizzle some olive oil into a non-stick frying pan and place over a medium heat.
3. Place the chorizo into the hot frying pan and sauté for a few minutes until crispy and the oil has melted out.
4. Place the sweet potatoes into the frying pan and stir them as they sauté for a few minutes; it's okay if you crush them a bit.
5. Add the spinach to the pan and stir into the sweet potatoes and chorizo until wilted.
6. Pour the egg over top of the sweet potato mixture and allow it to seep through the potatoes, make little holes with a wooden spoon to let the egg combine with the other ingredients if you need to.
7. Cook the hash for a few minutes or until the egg has just set.
8. Cut into 4 pieces and either store in one large container, or in 4 single-serve containers.
9. Place into the fridge to store until needed.
10. Eat hot or cold!

Blueberry and mint parfaits

Blueberries are full of antioxidants and healthy carbs. Not only are they nutritious, but they are tasty and pretty (for some reason I love to eat foods that look pretty on the plate, it makes it taste yummier somehow!). Mint is invigorating and refreshing, providing a burst of color. Of course, I have to add oats to the yoghurt-base of this parfait, they are too filling and wholesome to leave out.

Serves: 4 parfaits
Container: 4 glass bowls, ramekins, cups or airtight containers if transporting the parfait to work
Time: approximately 10 minutes

Nutritional info per serving:
- Calories: 272
- Fat: 8 grams
- Protein: 10 grams
- Carbs: 25 grams

Ingredients:
- 1 ½ cups wholegrain rolled oats
- 1 cup (8fl oz.) almond milk
- 2 cups (16fl oz.) unsweetened Greek yogurt
- 1 cup fresh blueberries (can also use frozen, no need to thaw first)
- 4 small fresh mint leaves, finely chopped

Method:
1. Place the oats and almond milk into a bowl and stir together to combine (this helps the oats to soften).
2. Spoon the oat and almond milk mixture evenly into your 4 containers.
3. Place a drop of yogurt into each container on top of the oats (use half of the yogurt as you'll be adding another layer of it).
4. Divide half of the blueberries between the 4 containers and sprinkle on top of the yogurt.
5. Add another layer of yogurt and then another layer of blueberries (you can use them all up at this stage).
6. Sprinkle the fresh mint over the top of each parfait.
7. Cover and place into the fridge to store until needed!

Peanut Butter and Banana Breakfast Cake

Do not panic, this is not a "cake" in the sense we usually think of cakes! As much as I would love to offer a regular cake for breakfast, it doesn't really help the weight loss cause. This "cake" contains bananas, peanut butter, eggs, almond flour and almond milk – healthy and nutritious ingredients full of energy, fat and protein. You can freeze slices of this and pull them out when you're in a pinch.

Serves: 8 slices (1 serving per slice)
Container: 1 large container or 8 single-serve containers if transporting to work
Time: approximately 20 minutes

Nutritional info per serving:
- Calories: 200
- Fat: 12 grams
- Protein: 7 grams
- Carbs: 16 grams

Ingredients:
- 3 bananas, mashed
- 4 tbsp. natural peanut butter (crunchy or smooth, either one is fine)
- 3 eggs
- 1 cup almond flour (this can be expensive so simply use whole-meal flour if you like)
- 1 cup (8fl oz.) almond milk
- 1 tsp. baking powder
- 1 tsp. vanilla extract

Method:
1. Preheat the oven to 356 degrees Fahrenheit and prepare a baking dish by lining with baking paper.
2. Place the bananas, peanut butter, eggs, almond flour, almond milk, baking powder and vanilla extract into a bowl and stir to combine.
3. Pour the mixture into the prepared baking dish and place into the oven, bake for approximately 15 minutes or until just set.
4. Leave to cool before slicing into 8 pieces and storing in an airtight container in the fridge.
5. Eat hot or cold!

Spinach and Zucchini Breakfast Pie with Optional Smoked Fish

Greens should ideally be consumed at every meal – they are the best source of essential micronutrients to keep you glowing and healthy. I have added "optional" smoked fish to this recipe because I understand that not everyone can stomach eating fish at breakfast time! Personally? I adore smoked trout so I always add it to this breakfast pie. Note: the nutritional information includes the smoked fish.

Serves: 8 slices (1 serving per slice)
Container: 1 large container or 8 single-serve containers if transporting to work
Time: approximately 25 minutes

Nutritional info per serving:
- Calories: 150
- Fat: 4 grams
- Protein: 11 grams
- Carbs: 10 grams

Ingredients:
- 3 cups baby spinach leaves, roughly chopped
- 2 large zucchinis, sliced
- 5 eggs, lightly beaten
- ½ cup (4floz) milk
- ½ cup whole-meal flour
- ½ tsp baking powder
- 7 oz. smoked fish, flaked (optional)
- Salt and pepper, to taste

Method:
1. Preheat the oven to 356 degrees Fahrenheit and prepare a baking tray by lining with baking paper.
2. Drizzle some olive oil into a frying pan and place over a medium heat.
3. Add the spinach and zucchini and sauté until wilted and softened.
4. In a bowl, whisk together the eggs, milk, flour and baking powder until smooth.
5. Add the cooked spinach, zucchini, and flaked smoke fish (if using) into the bowl and stir to combine, add a pinch of salt and pepper to season.
6. Pour into the prepared tray and place into the oven for approximately 15 minutes or until just set.
7. Leave to cool then cut into 8 pieces and store in the fridge!
8. Eat hot or cold.

Strawberry, Pumpkin Seed and Coconut Oat Baked Crisp

This is another "cake" inspired breakfast, but without the empty calories. Full of good fats and healthy fiber, this is a naturally sweet and tasty breakfast for eating on the go, or in a bowl with Greek yoghurt for more protein.

Serves: 8 slices (1 serving per slice)
Container: 1 large container or 8 single-serve containers if transporting to work
Time: approximately 25 minutes

Nutritional info per serving:
- Calories: 160
- Fat: 7 grams
- Protein: 7 grams
- Carbs: 19 grams

Ingredients:
- 3 tbsp. pumpkin seeds
- 2 cups wholegrain rolled oats
- ½ cup desiccated coconut
- 1 tsp. cinnamon
- 1 egg, lightly beaten
- 2 tbsp. honey
- ½ cup (4loz) almond milk
- ½ tsp. baking powder
- 1 cup fresh strawberries, stalks removed, cut into quarters

Method:
1. Preheat the oven to 356 degrees Fahrenheit and prepare a baking try by lining it with baking paper.
2. Place the pumpkin seeds, oats, coconut, cinnamon, egg, honey, almond milk and baking powder into a bowl and stir to combine; it will be thick – that's okay!
3. Press half of the mixture into the lined tray and then place the strawberries over the top in an even layer, press the rest of the oat mixture over top of the strawberries.
4. Place into the oven and bake for approximately 15 minutes or until golden.
5. Leave to cool before slicing into 8 pieces and storing in the fridge or freezer until needed!

Breakfast Tacos with Eggs, Bell Pepper and Mushrooms

I like to think of these breakfast tacos as something to make when I know I will have guests to cater to, who might like something a little more exciting than a regular breakfast. They are tasty and exciting, but still conform to the healthy-eating guidelines I have set for myself and my weight-loss goals. For low-carb days, just leave out the tortilla and have the eggs and veggies!

Serves: 8 tacos (2 tacos per serving, so 4 servings)
Container: you can store all 8 in one large container or use 4 smaller containers to store 2
Time: approximately 20 minutes

Nutritional info per serving:

- Calories: 387
- Fat: 15 grams
- Protein: 22 grams
- Carbs: 47 grams

Ingredients:

- 2 red bell peppers, core and seeds removed, flesh sliced
- 4 large Portobello mushrooms, sliced
- Salt and pepper, to taste
- 6 eggs, lightly beaten
- 8 whole-meal tortilla wraps
- 4 tbsp. plain Greek yogurt
- 1 fresh red chili, finely chopped
- Handful of fresh cilantro, roughly chopped

Method:

1. Drizzle some olive oil into a pan and place over a medium heat.
2. Add the bell peppers, mushrooms and a pinch of salt and pepper, sauté until soft.
3. Push the veggies to one side of the pan and pour the eggs on the other side, stirring and pushing them with a wooden spoon continuously as they scramble, cook until just set.
4. Take the pan off the heat and place your tortillas onto a large board or on a clean bench.

5. Spread a small amount of Greek yogurt onto each wrap, then divide and put the bell peppers and mushrooms between each wrap and place on top of the yogurt, then do the same with the egg between the wraps.
6. Finish with a sprinkle of chili and cilantro on top of each one!
7. Carefully fold them up and place them in your chosen containers.
8. Place into the fridge until needed!
9. These are best eaten cold due to the Greek yogurt addition.

Salmon, Kale, Ricotta and Egg Fry-pan Cake

Smoked salmon and ricotta are rich and full of good fats, so they can be eaten in small quantities in order to reap the benefits. Kale is, of course, full of minerals and fiber, and eggs are our protein savior.

Serves: 6 slices
Container: you can store all 6 slices in one container and take them out as you need them, or use 6 small containers if you are transporting the slices to work
Time: approximately 15 minutes

Nutritional info per serving:
- Calories: 120
- Fat: 7 grams
- Protein: 11 grams
- Carbs: 2 grams

Ingredients:
- 5 eggs, lightly beaten
- 4 oz. ricotta cheese
- 2 cups kale, finely sliced
- Salt and pepper, to taste
- 2 oz. smoked salmon, cut into small pieces

Method:
1. Place the eggs, ricotta, kale, salt and pepper into a bowl and whisk to combine.
2. Drizzle some olive oil into a non-stick fry pan and place over a medium heat.
3. Pour the egg mixture into the frying pan and sprinkle the smoked salmon pieces over the top.
4. Cook for approximately 7 minutes or until just set.
5. Leave to cool before slicing into 6 pieces and storing in the fridge until needed!

Healthy Breakfast Crumble with Stone Fruit and Berries

Yes, this is absolutely a fruit crumble – BUT, it doesn't have the flour, butter and sugar of a dessert crumble. Perfect for when stone fruits are in season! I use peaches and nectarines, but you could also use plums and any other yummy stone fruits you like. Be creative with the berries too, use a mixture!

Serves: 8 (small servings)
Container: I like to store the entire thing in a large airtight container and just take slices out when I need them, but you could divide them up and store in 8 small containers if you wish.
Time: approximately 35 minutes

Nutritional info per serving:
- Calories: 213
- Fat: 10 grams
- Protein: 5 grams
- Carbs: 31 grams

Ingredients:
- 3 ripe peaches, stones removed, flesh cut into slices
- 4 ripe nectarines, stones removed, flesh cut into slices
- 2 cups frozen mixed berries
- 1 ½ cups wholegrain rolled oats
- 1/3 cup sliced almonds
- 1 tbsp. chia seeds
- 1 tsp. cinnamon
- 1/3 cup desiccated coconut
- 2 tbsp. coconut oil
- 2 tbsp. honey

Method:
1. Preheat the oven to 356 degrees Fahrenheit.
2. Place the sliced peaches, nectarines and berries into a large rectangular baking dish and stir to combine.
3. Place the oats, almonds, chia seeds, cinnamon, desiccated coconut, coconut oil and honey into a bowl and stir to combine.
4. Sprinkle the crumble over the fruit and place into the oven to bake for approximately 30 minutes or until the crumble is golden and the fruit is soft.
5. Leave to cool before slicing into 8 slices and storing in the fridge until needed.

Lunch

These lunch recipes could also be used as dinner recipes, as they contain plenty of veggies and lean proteins. Grains such as quinoa and brown rice also feature in this section, as it's important to eat slow-releasing energy sources at lunchtime to keep you alert and full throughout the afternoon. If you are exercising a lot as part of your weight-loss attempts, then please don't forget to eat enough throughout the day! That means a wholesome lunch. You can go easy on the carbs at dinnertime if you wish, but don't be shy to chow down on plenty of nutrients for your midday meal.

Quinoa and Fresh Greens Salad

Many people assume that quinoa is a specialty ingredient, but it's so common these days it's just like rice or bread! It can be slightly pricey, but you don't need to use much. This salad is very simple: quinoa, lettuce, spinach, and green bell peppers, with a wee bit of feta to make it special.

Serves: 4
Container: you will need 4 airtight containers or lunchboxes
Time: approximately 25 minutes

Nutritional info per serving:
- Calories: 450
- Fat: 9 grams
- Protein: 17 grams
- Carbs: 65 grams

Ingredients:
- 1 cup dry quinoa
- 1 ½ cups (12floz) salt-reduced chicken broth/stock
- 3 cups shredded lettuce (use any, I use iceberg)
- 2 cups baby spinach leaves
- 2 green bell peppers, core and seeds removed, sliced
- 3 oz. feta cheese, cut into small chunks
- Salt and pepper, to taste

Method:
1. Thoroughly rinse the quinoa in a sieve to remove the bitter outer layer.
2. Bring the chicken broth to the boil in a small pot and add the quinoa, stir to combine then turn the heat down to a simmer, cover, and cook for 12-15 minutes or until the liquid has disappeared and the quinoa is soft.
3. Divide the cooked quinoa between your 4 containers, then divide the lettuce, spinach, bell peppers and feta between the containers and place on top of the quinoa.
4. Sprinkle with salt and pepper and a drizzle of olive oil to finish.
5. Cover and place into the fridge until needed!

Roasted Veggie Salad

Easy, classic, tasty and filling. A roasted veggie salad is what I turn to when all I want to do is throw a tray in the oven and be done with it! Added seeds provide extra fats and energy.

Serves: 4
Container: you will need 4 airtight containers
Time: approximately 30 minutes

Nutritional info per serving:
- Calories: 300
- Fat: 16 grams
- Protein: 9 grams
- Carbs: 31 grams

Ingredients:
- 2 cups cubed butternut squash (I keep the skin on but you can remove it if you wish)
- 2 cups cubed sweet potato
- 2 carrots, chopped into chunks
- 2 large Portobello mushrooms, thickly sliced
- 2 large zucchinis, cut into chunks
- 1 head of broccoli, cut into florets
- 2 tbsp. sunflower seeds
- 2 tbsp. pumpkin seeds
- 3 tbsp. olive oil (I've added the oil in here because it's quite a lot and it adjusts the calorie count)
- Salt and pepper, to taste

Method:
1. Preheat the oven to 356 degrees Fahrenheit and prepare a tray by lining it with baking paper.
2. Place all ingredients onto the tray and add a sprinkle of salt and pepper.
3. Combine the ingredients together with your hands, making sure everything gets coated in olive oil.
4. Place into the oven and bake for approximately 30 minutes or until the veggies are soft and the seeds are toasted.
5. Divide into your 4 containers, cover and place into the fridge until needed.

Grilled Chicken with Sweet Potatoes and Asparagus

Lean protein and healthy carbs – a lunch of champions. It's simple, yes, but it is delicious. High-energy days with weight training call for a lunch just like this one. You only need an oven and one tray to complete this dish!

Serves: 4
Container: you will need 4 airtight containers
Time: approximately 35 minutes

Nutritional info per serving:

- Calories: 280
- Fat: 13 grams
- Protein: 28 grams
- Carbs: 11 grams

Ingredients:

- 4 small chicken breasts
- 1 large sweet potato, cut into chunks
- 16 spears of asparagus, tough ends removed
- 2 tbsp. olive oil
- 1 tsp. dried rosemary
- Salt and pepper, to taste

Method:

1. Preheat the oven to 356 degrees Fahrenheit and prepare a tray by lining it with baking paper.
2. Place the chicken, sweet potato, asparagus, olive oil, rosemary, salt and pepper onto the tray and combine with your hands until everything is coated in oil and seasoning.
3. Place into the oven and bake for approximately 30 minutes or until the chicken is cooked through and the sweet potatoes are soft.
4. Divide between your 4 containers, cover, and place into the fridge until needed.
5. Eat hot or cold!

Brown Rice and Tuna Bowls

Brown rice and canned tuna – a student's dream! Affordable and nutritious, this is a lunch for tight budgets and energetic days. Best eaten cold for a Summery and refreshing lunchtime munch.

Serves: 4
Container: you will need 4 airtight containers
Time: approximately 25 minutes

Nutritional info per serving:
- Calories: 450
- Fat: 5 grams
- Protein: 23 grams
- Carbs: 78 grams

Ingredients:
- 2 cups dry brown rice
- 4 small cans of unflavored tuna (the single-serve cans)
- 1 carrot, peeled and chopped into small pieces
- 1 red bell pepper, core and seeds removed, cut into small pieces
- 1 cup chopped cucumber
- 1 tbsp. balsamic vinegar

Method:
1. Place the brown rice into a pot and add 3 ½ cups of water and a pinch of salt, bring to the boil then reduce to a simmer, leave covered until the water has disappeared and the rice is soft (but still with a bite!).
2. Divide the cooked rice between your 4 containers and add the contents of one tuna can into each, divide the carrot, bell pepper, cucumber and balsamic vinegar between the 4 containers and stir to combine with the rice.
3. Cover and place into the fridge to store until needed!

Pita Pockets with Lamb and Salad

Whole-meal pita pockets with lamb and salad greens, with a drizzle of plain yoghurt. This is the kind of lunch you'll want to eat as soon as you get to work! But you'll just have to wait.

Serves: 4
Container: you will need 4 airtight containers
Time: approximately 20 minutes

Nutritional info per serving:

- Calories: 520
- Fat: 27 grams
- Protein: 37 grams
- Carbs: 32 grams

Ingredients:

- 12 oz. lamb steaks, cut into cubes
- 1 tsp. ground cumin
- Salt and pepper, to taste
- 4 whole-meal pita breads
- 2 cups salad greens (mixed kale, lettuce and arugula is ideal)
- 4 tbsp. plain yogurt
- 1 lemon, cut into quarters

Method:

1. Drizzle some olive oil into a fry pan and place over a medium heat.
2. Add the lamb, cumin, salt and pepper and stir to combine, sauté for about 7 minutes or until the lamb cubes are cooked but still a little pink.
3. Make a slit in each pita bread and fill each one with mixed salad greens, lamb, and a drizzle of yogurt.
4. Place the filled pitas into your 4 containers and place a lemon quarter in each one so you can squeeze it over the pita when you're ready to eat!
5. Cover the containers and store in the fridge until needed.

Sticky Chicken and Broccoli Prep Bowls

Chicken and broccoli – the dieters staple! But this dish is far from bland or boring. Soy sauce and honey make a sticky sauce for the chicken, and sesame oil jazzes-up the broccoli for a tasty and filling lunch suitable for any day of the week.

Serves: 4
Container: you will need 4 airtight containers
Time: approximately 30 minutes

Nutritional info per serving:
Calories: 298
Fat: 12 grams
Protein: 31 grams
Carbs: 19 grams

Ingredients:
- 2 tbsp. honey
- 2 tsp. soy sauce (tamari is best)
- 4 boneless, skinless chicken thighs
- 1 head of broccoli, cut into florets
- 1 tsp. sesame oil

Method:
1. Drizzle some olive oil into a frying pan and place over a medium heat.
2. Add the honey and soy sauce, place the chicken thighs into the pan and stir to coat in soy and honey, sauté for approximately 15 minutes or until the chicken is almost cooked.
3. Add the broccoli to the pan, increase the heat to high, splash a few teaspoons of water into the pan and immediate place a lid onto the pan – this will steam the broccoli.
4. Once the water has evaporated, remove the lid and check that the chicken has cooked through and the broccoli is cooked yet crunchy.
5. Drizzle the sesame oil over the broccoli before dividing the chicken and broccoli between your 4 containers.
6. Cover and store in the fridge until needed!

Tuna, Corn, and Cheese Hot Sandwiches (for cheat days and cravings)

I just had to add a recipe in here which was just a teeny, tiny bit naughty. After all, a cheat meal here and there is not going to ruin your weight loss! This recipe is still tasty and uses whole, real ingredients, but it's quite bread and cheese-rich, so it's definitely one to keep up your sleeve until you're really craving some comfort food. Prepare the sandwiches the night/s before, then throw them on the grill or in the sandwich press before eating.

Serves: 4
Container: you will need 4 airtight containers
Time: approximately 15 minutes

Nutritional info per serving:

- Calories: 380
- Fat: 14 grams
- Protein: 21 grams
- Carbs: 36 grams

Ingredients:

- 4 slices of cheddar cheese
- 8 slices of wholegrain bread
- 1 cup corn kernels, fresh or canned
- 2 small cans of tuna (single-serve cans, half a can per sandwich)
- Salt and pepper, to taste

Method:

1. Place a slice of cheese onto 4 of your bread slices, top with corn kernels and tuna, sprinkle with salt and pepper then place the other slice of bread on top of each sandwich.
2. Wrap in plastic wrap to keep the sandwiches together and place into your airtight containers.
3. Store in the fridge until need, and place into a hot sandwich press to toast before eating!

Stuffed Sweet Potatoes

By now you will have noticed that sweet potatoes are cropping up a LOT in this recipe book! But I think they are too good not to take advantage of. These sweet potatoes are stuffed with scallions, parsley, a little cottage cheese, and some baby spinach.

Serves: 4
Container: you will need 4 airtight containers
Time: approximately 20 minutes

Nutritional info per serving:
- Calories: 190
- Fat: 3 grams
- Protein: 9 grams
- Carbs: 27 grams

Ingredients:
- 4 sweet potatoes, pricked all over with a fork
- 1 scallion, finely chopped
- Small handful of parsley, finely chopped
- 1 cup cottage cheese
- 1 cup baby spinach leaves
- Salt and pepper, to taste

Method:
1. Place the sweet potatoes into the microwave and cook on HIGH for 1 minute increments until soft all the way through.
2. Cut the sweet potatoes in half and remove the flesh and place it into a small bowl.
3. Add the scallions, parsley, cottage cheese, spinach, salt and pepper, stir to combine.
4. Re-fill the sweet potato skins with the filling and place 2 halves into each of your 4 containers.
5. Place into the fridge to store until needed!

Homemade Hummus, Tomato, and Ham Rice Wafer Stacks

This is a light, "snacky" lunch for when you feel like nibbling rather than feasting. Rice wafers, tomato, ham and delicious homemade hummus – all with a sprinkle of salt and pepper. Delicious.

Serves: 4
Container: you will need 4 airtight containers, containers with separate compartments would be ideal!
Time: approximately 20 minutes

Nutritional info per serving:
- Calories: 340
- Fat: 19 grams
- Protein: 12 grams
- Carbs: 32 grams

Ingredients:
- 1 can of chickpeas, drained
- 1 tbsp. tahini
- 1 garlic clove
- 4 tbsp. olive oil
- 1 lemon
- Salt and pepper, to taste
- 12 rice wafers
- 2 large tomatoes, sliced
- 4 large slices of deli ham

Method:
1. Make the hummus by placing the chickpeas, tahini, garlic clove, olive oil, juice of one lemon, salt and pepper into a blender or food processor and blending until smooth.
2. Wrap your rice wafers in plastic wrap to keep them fresh and place them into the pantry.
3. Place a good drop of hummus into one corner of your airtight containers, then divide the tomato and ham between the containers too.
4. Place the lid onto your containers and place them into the fridge until needed.
5. When it's time to pack your lunch into your work bag, simply place a container of toppings into your bag and grab a packet of wrapped rice wafers too.
6. Assemble just before eating for a fresh and crunchy lunch!

Grilled Salmon and Seasonal Greens

Fresh salmon isn't always the most affordable ingredient, but treat yourself do a few salmon lunches every few weeks. The protein and fatty acids are so worth the money spent! Use any seasonal greens you have; this recipe uses broccoli and zucchini.

Serves: 4
Container: you will need 4 airtight containers
Time: approximately 30 minutes

Nutritional info per serving:
Calories: 235
Fat: 7 grams
Protein: 30 grams
Carbs: 13 grams

Ingredients:
- 4 small-medium salmon filets
- Salt and pepper, to taste
- Olive oil
- 1 head of broccoli, cut into florets
- 2 large zucchinis, chopped into chunks
- 1 tsp. sesame oil

Method:
1. Preheat the oven to 356 degrees Fahrenheit and line a baking tray with baking paper, place the salmon filets onto the tray and sprinkle with salt, pepper and a little olive oil.
2. Place into the oven and bake for approximately 12 minutes or until cooked to your liking.
3. As the salmon cooks, prepare the greens by placing a pot of water over a high heat and bringing to the boil, place a steaming basket or double boiler over the pot and place the greens inside, place the lid onto the basket.
4. Steam the veggies for a few minutes until just cooked, sprinkle with the sesame oil and some salt and pepper.
5. Place a salmon filet into each container and divide the veggies between each container.
6. Place the lid onto each container and place into the fridge to store before serving.
7. Eat hot or cold!

Chicken, strawberry, and black rice salad

Black rice is a bit more exciting than regular rice, and the addition of strawberries makes it even more exotic! Even though it sounds a bit strange and fancy, it's really not. Black rice is available at most supermarkets, as are strawberries in the right season! Grilled chicken is gently seasoned with lemon, salt and pepper.

Serves: 4
Container: you will need 4 airtight containers
Time: approximately 40 minutes

Nutritional info per serving:
- Calories: 380
- Fat: 3 grams
- Protein: 14 grams
- Carbs: 68 grams

Ingredients:
- 2 cups dry black rice
- 1 large chicken breast
- Olive oil
- Salt and pepper, to taste
- 1 cup strawberries, stalks removed, sliced
- 1 lemon

Method:
1. Preheat the oven to 356 degrees Fahrenheit and line a baking tray with baking paper.
2. Place the rice into a pot and add 4 cups of water and a pinch of salt, bring to the boil then reduce to a simmer, cover and let simmer until the water has disappeared and the rice is cooked.
3. While the rice is cooking, cook the chicken by placing it onto the lined baking tray, drizzling with olive oil, and sprinkling with salt and pepper, bake in the preheated oven for approximately 20 minutes or until cooked through.
4. Shred the cooked chicken breast and add to the pot with the cooked black rice.
5. Place the strawberries into the pot and squeeze in the juice of one lemon.
6. Season with salt and pepper before stirring to combine.
7. Divide between your 4 containers, cover and store in the fridge until needed!

Smoked Salmon and Avocado Wholegrain Wraps

Smoked salmon and avocado, wrapped in a soft and healthy wholegrain wrap, with lots of crispy lettuce and a drizzle of vinegar dressing.

Serves: 4
Container: you will need 4 airtight containers
Time: approximately 20 minutes

Nutritional info per serving:
- Calories: 365
- Fat: 20 grams
- Protein: 10 grams
- Carbs: 37 grams

Ingredients:
- 4 wholegrain wraps
- 2 cups lettuce, roughly sliced
- 2 avocadoes, flesh sliced
- 3 oz. smoked salmon
- Olive oil
- 1 tbsp. balsamic vinegar mixed with 1 tablespoon of olive oil

Method:
1. Place your wraps onto a large board or clean bench.
2. Place a pile of lettuce onto each one, then add ½ an avocado (sliced) on top, place the salmon on top of the avocado and drizzle with olive oil and vinegar.
3. Carefully wrap your wraps into tight parcels, place into your containers and store in the fridge until needed.

Cold Tuna and Pasta Salad

There's only a small amount of whole-meal pasta in this recipe, just enough to fill you up! Tuna, avocado, carrot, corn and bell peppers bulk-out the veggie quota for this yummy cold salad.

Serves: 4
Container: you will need 4 airtight containers
Time: approximately 30 minutes

Nutritional info per serving:
- Calories: 235
- Fat: 10 grams
- Protein: 10 grams
- Carbs: 28 grams

Ingredients:
- 1 ½ cups whole-meal penne pasta (or any other shapes you have handy!)
- 2 cans tuna (the single-serve cans) drained
- 2 carrots, peeled and cut into small pieces
- ¾ cup corn kernels
- 1 avocado, flesh cut into chunks
- 1 red bell pepper, core and seeds removed, flesh cut into small pieces
- Salt and pepper, to taste

Method:
1. Bring a pot of water to boil and add pinch of salt and the dry pasta, cook until the pasta is al dente (some pastas differ so use the instructions on your packet).
2. Drain the pasta and leave to cool slightly before adding the tuna, carrots, corn, avocado, bell pepper, salt, pepper and a drizzle of olive oil.
3. Divide the pasta salad between your 4 containers, cover and place into the fridge to store until needed.
4. Serve cold!

Cauliflower Rice and Chili Chicken

Cauliflower rice is an angel-sent food or anyone wanting to lower their carb intake. It's affordable, easy, tasty and low in calories. Chicken rubbed with chili and olive oil, baked in the oven to moist perfection!

Serves: 4
Container: you will need 4 airtight containers
Time: approximately 30 minutes

Nutritional info per serving:
- Calories: 310
- Fat: 21 grams
- Protein: 21 grams
- Carbs: 12 grams

Ingredients:
- 1 head of cauliflower, core removed, florets cut into chunks
- Salt and pepper, to taste
- 4 boneless, skinless chicken thighs
- 2 tbsp. olive oil
- 1 fresh red chili, finely chopped
- 1 garlic clove, crushed
- 1 lemon, cut into quarters

Method:
1. Preheat the oven to 356 degrees Fahrenheit and line a baking tray with baking paper.
2. Place the cauliflower into a food processor and blend until it resembles the size and consistency of rice.
3. Place the cauliflower into a bowl and sprinkle with salt and pepper, place in the microwave and cook on HIGH for 1 minute increments until cooked through.
4. Place the chicken thighs onto the lined baking tray and sprinkle the olive oil, chili, garlic, salt and pepper on top rub to combine and make sure the chicken is well-coated.
5. Place the chicken into the preheated oven and bake for approximately 20 minutes or until the chicken is cooked through.
6. Divide the cauliflower rice between the 4 containers and place a chicken thigh into each container on top of the "rice".
7. Place a lemon quarter into each container, cover and place into the fridge until needed!

Loaded Broccoli Salad with Toasted Seeds

More broccoli! As you can see, I put broccoli in a huge portion of my meals. The fiber, nutrients and vitamins broccoli provides are potently perfect. Toasted seeds, red onion, and Parmesan cheese add a unique twist to this green and glorious salad.

Serves: 4
Container: you will need 4 airtight containers
Time: approximately 20 minutes

Nutritional info per serving:
- Calories: 195
- Fat: 14 grams
- Protein: 11 grams
- Carbs: 12 grams

Ingredients:
- Olive oil
- 1 large head of broccoli, stalk removed, cut into florets
- ¼ red onion, finely chopped
- 2 tbsp. pumpkin seeds
- 2 tbsp. sunflower seeds
- 3 tbsp. grated Parmesan cheese
- Salt and pepper, to taste

Method:
1. Drizzle some olive oil into a frying pan and place over a medium heat.
2. Add the broccoli and sauté for a few minutes.
3. Pour a few tablespoons of water into the pan and immediately place a lid on top to trap the steam, this will steam the broccoli.
4. Once the water has evaporated and the broccoli is cooked but still has a "bite", add the red onion, pumpkin seeds and sunflower seeds, continue cooking for about 1 minute until the seeds are gently toasted.
5. Divide the broccoli mixture between your 4 containers and sprinkle the Parmesan over each one.
6. Finish with a sprinkle of salt and pepper and a little drizzle of olive oil.
7. Cover and place into the fridge until needed!

White Bean and Tomato Salad with Balsamic Dressing

This salad reminds me of a sundrenched afternoon in Italy. Beans should never be overlooked, they are a dieter's best friend, in my humble opinion. Gluten-free, filling, fibrous and can be put into many different dishes, beans are the best! This salad utilizes white beans, fresh tomatoes, basil and balsamic vinegar.

Serves: 4
Container: you will need 4 airtight containers
Time: approximately 10 minutes

Nutritional info per serving:
- Calories: 250
- Fat: 7 grams
- Protein: 13 grams
- Carbs: 33 grams

Ingredients:
- 2 cans white beans, drained
- 3 ripe tomatoes, cut into chunks
- Small handful of fresh basil, roughly chopped
- 2 tbsp. balsamic vinegar mixed with 2 tablespoons of olive oil
- Salt and pepper, to taste

Method:
1. Place the beans, tomatoes, basil, balsamic, olive oil, salt and pepper into a small bowl and mix to combine.
2. Divide into your 4 containers, cover and place into the fridge to store until needed.
3. Eat cold!

Basil, Tomato and Haloumi Salad with Cos and Cucumber

Another recipe with basil and tomato, the combination is so tasty it should be enjoyed as often as possible. Salty haloumi cheese satisfies the palate, while lettuce and cucumber refreshes and nourishes you.

Serves: 4
Container: you will need 4 airtight containers
Time: approximately 20 minutes

Nutritional info per serving:
- Calories: 250
- Fat: 20 grams
- Protein: 11 grams
- Carbs: 8 grams

Ingredients:
- 7 oz. halloumi cheese, sliced into 12 slices
- 2 cos or Romaine lettuces, roughly chopped
- 1 cup chopped cucumber
- 3 large tomatoes, sliced
- Large handful of fresh basil, roughly chopped
- 2 tbsp. apple cider vinegar mixed with 2 tbsp. olive oil

Method:
1. Heat a non-stick frying pan over a high heat.
2. Add the halloumi slices to the pan and cook on both sides until golden.
3. Divide the lettuce, cucumber, tomatoes, basil, and halloumi between the 4 containers.
4. Sprinkle with salt and pepper and the oil/vinegar mixture, gently toss to combine and coat with dressing.
5. Cover and place into the fridge to store until needed.

Prepped Topping Packs for Rice Wafers

A variety of toppings for rice wafers, neatly packed away in a container until you're ready to DIY your rice wafers for a tasty and healthy lunch. The nutritional information includes all of the toppings plus 4 plain rice wafers. I LOVE to spread peanut butter onto rice wafers and then slice quarter of a banana over top for a savory-sweet treat.

Serves: 4
Container: you will need 4 airtight containers, preferably with separated compartments
Time: approximately 10 minutes

Nutritional info per serving:
- Calories: 310
- Fat: 11 grams
- Protein: 19 grams
- Carbs: 36 grams

Ingredients:
- 1 cup cottage cheese
- 4 tbsp. chopped chives
- 1 fresh tomato, sliced
- 4 slices of deli ham or turkey
- 4 tbsp. peanut butter
- 1 banana, cut into 4 chunks
- (plus 4 rice wafers per lunch serving)

Method:
1. Place the cottage cheese, chives, tomato, ham or turkey, peanut butter, and banana into a container with separated compartments.
2. Cover and place into the fridge to store until needed.
3. Wrap the rice wafers in sealable bags or plastic wrap, or keep them in an airtight container at work to pull out whenever you need them!

Minced Lamb Meat Balls with Yogurt and Cucumber Dip

Meatballs for lunch? Yes! Lamb, yoghurt and cucumber is a refreshing and Greek-inspired combination. You could serve with a pita bread for extra carbs if you've had, or have got a big workout ahead of you!

Serves: 4
Container: you will need 4 airtight containers
Time: approximately 25 minutes

Nutritional info per serving:
- Calories: 390
- Fat: 26 grams
- Protein: 31 grams
- Carbs: 4 grams

Ingredients:
- 17.5 oz. minced lamb
- ½ red onion, finely chopped
- 1 egg
- ½ cup almond flour
- Salt and pepper, to taste
- Olive oil
- ½ cup plain Greek yogurt
- ¾ cup finely chopped cucumber

Method:
1. Place the minced lamb, red onion, egg, almond flour, salt and pepper into a bowl and stir to combine.
2. Drizzle some olive oil into a non-stick fry pan and place over a medium heat.
3. Roll the lamb mixture into 16 balls and place them in 2 batches into the hot pan, cook for about 7 minutes, turning a few times until golden and cooked through.
4. Stir together the yogurt and cucumber in a small bowl.
5. Place 4 lamb balls into each container and place a drop of yogurt mixture over top.
6. Cover and place into the fridge to store until needed.
7. Eat cold or hot! (Place the yogurt on the side if you want to eat the lamb balls hot, so then you don't have to heat the yogurt as well).

One-Tray Chicken Thigh and Root Veggie Baked "Bowls"

Another chicken and veggie dish! As mentioned before, you can't really go wrong with chicken and veggies when you are trying to trim down. The veggies in question here are root veggies: carrots, parsnips, beets and onions – filling, fibrous and full of minerals.

Serves: 4
Container: you will need 4 airtight containers or bowls
Time: approximately 35 minutes

Nutritional info per serving:
- Calories: 360
- Fat: 17 grams
- Protein: 29 grams
- Carbs: 23 grams

Ingredients:
- 4 boneless, skinless chicken thighs
- 2 carrots, cut into small chunks
- 2 parsnips, peeled and cut into chunks
- 2 raw beets, cut into chunks
- 1 large red onion, cut into wedges
- 1 tsp. mixed dried herbs
- Olive oil
- Salt and pepper, to taste
- 1 lemon, cut into quarters

Method:
1. Preheat the oven to 356 degrees Fahrenheit and line a baking tray with baking paper.
2. Place the chicken thighs, carrots, parsnips, beets, onion, herbs and a drizzle of olive oil onto the tray, add a pinch of salt and pepper and combine all of the ingredients with your hands.
3. Place the tray into the oven and bake for approximately 30 minutes or until the chicken is cooked through and the veggies are soft.
4. Divide the chicken and veggies between the 4 containers and place a lemon quarter into each container.
5. Place into the fridge to store until needed!

Cold Soba Noodle Salad with Cashews, Carrot and Tofu

Soba noodles are available at all Asian supermarkets. They are affordable, tasty, and if you get the 100% buckwheat variety, they are gluten free. Cashews and carrot for flavor and crunch, and tofu for protein and flavor-soaking goodness.

Serves: 4
Container: you will need 4 airtight containers
Time: approximately 20 minutes

Nutritional info per serving:
- Calories: 490
- Fat: 10 grams
- Protein: 22 grams
- Carbs: 87 grams

Ingredients:
- 14 oz. dry soba noodles
- 2 tbsp. sesame oil
- 2 tbsp. soy sauce
- 1 tbsp. honey
- 9 oz. firm tofu, sliced
- 1/3 cup raw cashew nuts
- 2 carrots, peeled and chopped into small pieces

Method:
1. Place a pot of water over a high heat, bring to the boil and add the soba noodles, cook until soft.
2. While the noodles are cooking, drizzle the sesame oil, soy sauce and honey into a small non-stick fry pan and place over a medium heat.
3. Place the tofu slices into the hot pan and cook for a couple of minutes on each side until golden.
4. Drain the noodles and place into a bowl.
5. Add the cashews, carrots, and cooked tofu with any oil/soy sauce left over in the fry pan.
6. Stir to combine.
7. Divide into your 4 containers, cover and place into the fridge to store until needed!
8. Best eaten cold!

Dinner

I find that dinner time is the worst time when it comes to stress and rushing. Therefore, it's important to MEGA-prep your dinners. I'm talking a freezer full of meals you can whip out in the morning or the night before and leave in the fridge to thaw in time for dinner. In this section, you will find prepped pasta sauces and prepped marinated meats to store in the freezer. Marinating meat and making sauces is usually the most time-consuming part of dinner, so get the hard part out of the way well in advance!

Freezer Soup (Pumpkin and Coconut)

Keeping soup in the freezer, stored in single-serve containers is a very smart move indeed. This pumpkin and coconut soup freezes really well and it's filling enough to satisfy you, but light enough to enjoy during any season. Super low in calories, so you can add a piece of buttered toast and not ruin your diet (well, that's my logic anyway!).

Serves: 6
Container: you will need 6 airtight, freezer-safe containers
Time: approximately 45 minutes

Nutritional info per serving:
- Calories: 105
- Fat: 4 grams
- Protein: 5 grams
- Carbs: 16 grams

Ingredients:
- 6 cups cubed pumpkin (skin removed, about 1 medium-sized pumpkin)
- 1 onion, finely chopped
- 2 carrots, cut into chunks
- 3 cups (24fl oz.) chicken stock
- Salt and pepper, to taste
- 1 cup (8fl oz.) coconut milk

Method:
1. Place the pumpkin, onion, carrots, stock, salt and pepper into a pot and bring to the boil, reduce to a simmer and simmer covered for about 25 minutes or until the veggies are soft.
2. Using a hand-held stick blender, blend until smooth.
3. Stir the coconut milk into the soup, taste, and add more salt and pepper if needed.
4. Allow it to cool slightly before pouring into your 6 containers, covering, then packing away into the freezer!
5. Remember to label the containers with masking tape and a sharpie so you can keep track of when the soup was made.
6. Simply take out of the freezer the morning of the day you want to have the soup for dinner, and leave to thaw on the kitchen bench.
7. Throw it into a pot or place into the microwave in a bowl to heat.

Spicy Lentil Stew with Sweet Potato Mash and Cilantro

This is a total Winter dream dinner dish. I recommend making some servings of this stew and mash and keeping them in the freezer. Super easy, affordable, filling, and nourishing. Add as much chili as you like, according to your spice preference!

Serves: 6
Container: you will need 6 airtight containers
Time: approximately 40 minutes

Nutritional info per serving:
- Calories: 270
- Fat: 5 grams
- Protein: 19 grams
- Carbs: 34 grams

Ingredients:
- Olive oil
- 1 onion, finely chopped
- 1 tsp. cumin
- 1 tsp. chili powder
- 1 tsp. ground coriander
- 1 can (14 oz.) chopped tomatoes
- 2 cans (14 oz.) brown lentils, drained
- Salt and pepper, to taste
- 1 cup (8fl oz.) chicken stock
- 2 large sweet potatoes, cut into cubes
- Large handful of cilantro, roughly chopped

Method:
1. Drizzle some olive oil into a pot and place over a medium heat.
2. Add the onion, cumin, chili, ground coriander, tomatoes, lentils, salt and pepper, stir to combine.
3. Add chicken stock to the pot.
4. Allow it to simmer for about 20 minutes until thick and rich.

5. As the lentil stew simmers, cook the sweet potatoes by pricking all over with a fork and cooking in the microwave on HIGH for 1 minute increments until soft all the way through.

6. Cut the cooked sweet potatoes into chunks and place into a bowl (I keep the skin on, it has nutrients!), add some salt and pepper and mash with a fork.

7. Divide the sweet potato mash between your 6 containers then divide the lentil stew between the containers and spoon on top of the sweet potatoes.

8. Sprinkle with fresh cilantro, cover and place into the fridge or freezer (or both, freeze 3, fridge 3!) until needed.

Rainbow Chicken Salad

The "rainbow" comes from the beautiful array of colors in this fresh and yummy salad. Red cabbage, carrot, cucumber, yellow bell peppers, lettuce and tomatoes burst onto the plate, with tender chicken. Make a big bowl of this on your meal-prep day and eat it for dinner for 3 nights after.

Serves: 6 (enough for 3 nights for 2 people)
Container: you will need one large airtight container or 6 smaller airtight containers
Time: approximately 30 minutes

Nutritional info per serving:
- Calories: 205
- Fat: 6 grams
- Protein: 22 grams
- Carbs: 15 grams

Ingredients:
- 2 chicken breasts
- Olive oil
- Salt and pepper, to taste
- ½ head of red cabbage, thinly sliced
- 2 carrots, grated
- 1 cup cubed cucumber
- 2 yellow bell peppers, core and seeds removed, thinly sliced
- ½ head iceberg lettuce, roughly chopped
- 2 tomatoes, chopped into chunks
- 2 tbsp. balsamic vinegar mixed with 2 tbsp. olive oil

Method:
1. Preheat the oven to 356 degrees Fahrenheit and line a baking tray with baking paper.
2. Place the chicken breasts onto the tray and rub with olive oil, salt and pepper, place into the oven and bake for approximately 25 minutes or until cooked all the way through.
3. Slice the cooked chicken breasts into thin slices.

4. Place the cabbage, carrot, cucumber, bell peppers, lettuce, tomatoes, balsamic vinegar, olive oil and chicken into a large bowl and gently toss to combine and coat in oil and vinegar.
5. Divide the salad between your 6 containers, cover and place into the fridge to store until needed!
6. Eat within 3 nights of cooking (3 dinners for 2 people).

Veggie Stacks with Feta and Mint

There's so much fresh mint in my garden at the moment I am finding myself adding it to so many of my recipes and meals! It goes so well with feta cheese, and just as well with veggies. These stacks feature mushrooms, zucchini, eggplant, and tomato.

Serves: 4
Container: you will need 4 airtight containers
Time: approximately 25 minutes

Nutritional info per serving:
- Calories: 230
- Fat: 12 grams
- Protein: 10 grams
- Carbs: 18 grams

Ingredients:
- 8 large Portobello mushrooms
- 2 large zucchinis, sliced lengthways
- 1 large eggplant, sliced into 8 slices
- 2 large tomatoes, sliced
- 2 tbsp. olive oil
- 2 garlic cloves, crushed
- Salt and pepper, to taste
- 3.5 oz. feta cheese
- Small handful fresh mint leaves

Method:
1. Preheat the oven to 356 degrees Fahrenheit and line a baking tray with baking paper.
2. Lay the mushrooms, zucchini slices, eggplant slices, and tomato slices onto the tray and drizzle over the olive oil, garlic, salt and pepper.
3. Place the tray into the oven and bake for approximately 20 minutes until tender and golden.
4. Create your stacks by layering in this order: mushrooms, feta, zucchini slices, feta, eggplant slices, mint, tomato slices, feta, mint.
5. Place a skewer through the middle of each stack to keep them together if you like!
6. Pack away into your containers, cover and place into the fridge until needed.

Lamb and Red Onion Skewers

These skewers have two core ingredients: lamb and red onion. You can make a big batch of these and add any salad to go with it.

Serves: 8 skewers (2 skewers per serving, so 4 servings)
Container: store in one large, airtight container and take them out as you need them
Time: approximately 25 minutes

Nutritional info per serving:

Calories: 270
Fat: 19 grams
Protein: 27 grams
Carbs: 4 grams

Ingredients:

- 4 lamb leg steaks, cut into cubes
- 2 red onions, cut into 6 wedges each
- 2 tbsp. olive oil
- Salt and pepper, to taste
- 8 skewers

Method:

1. Preheat the oven to 400 degrees Fahrenheit and line a baking tray with baking paper.
2. Load the skewers by alternating lamb and onion until full (but leave an inch on either side of the skewers so you can pick them up easily).
3. Rub the onion and lamb with olive oil and sprinkle with salt and pepper and place on the tray.
4. Place the tray into the oven and bake for approximately 20 minutes, turning once, until the onions are cooked and beginning to turn golden, and the lamb is cooked but still pink inside.
5. Leave the skewers to cool slightly before packing away into a large container, covering and storing in the fridge until needed.

Veggie Burgers Patties

These veggie burger patties can be eaten with a simple salad, or turned into a delicious burger with a wholegrain bun, tomato, lettuce, relish and mustard. The nutritional information provided is for the patties only. These patties are cooked in the oven which eliminates the need for oil, and therefore, less calories.

Serves: makes 8 large patties
Container: store in one airtight container and take them out as you need them, you can also freeze them too, wrap them individually in greaseproof paper so they don't stick together in the container
Time: approximately 25 minutes

Nutritional info per serving: Per patty
- Calories: 130
- Fat: 4 grams
- Protein: 7 grams
- Carbs: 14 grams

Ingredients:
- 5 Portobello mushrooms, cut into small pieces
- 1 cup corn kernels
- 1 cup chickpeas, drained and rinsed
- 2 eggs, lightly beaten
- 1 cup almond flour
- Large handful of fresh parsley, finely chopped
- 1 tsp. ground cumin
- 1 tsp. ground coriander
- 1 tsp. chili powder
- Salt and pepper, to taste

Method:
1. Preheat the oven to 356 degrees Fahrenheit and line a baking tray with baking paper.
2. Place all ingredients into a large bowl and add a pinch of salt and pepper.
3. Vigorously stir until thoroughly combined.
4. Shape the mixture into 8 large patties.
5. Place the patties onto the baking tray and place into the oven.
6. Bake for about 7 minutes on each side (just take the tray out of the oven and turn the patties over after 7 minutes then put them back in for another 7) or until cooked through and golden on the outside.
7. Stack into an airtight container and store in the fridge until needed.

Mexican-Inspired Shepherd's Pie

Black beans, cilantro, chili and sweet potatoes make up the bulk of this yummy shepherd's pie with a Mexican twist. Make a big dish of it, cut it into servings, and throw it in the fridge or freezer for dinners all week long!

Serves: 1 large pie with 8 servings
Container: store in one large container or 8 single-serve containers if freezing for single portions
Time: approximately 45 minutes

Nutritional info per serving:
- Calories: 210
- Fat: 5 grams
- Protein: 18 grams
- Carbs: 21 grams

Ingredients:
- Olive oil
- 1 onion, finely chopped
- 17 oz. minced beef
- 2 cans (14 oz.) black beans, drained
- 1 tsp. chili powder
- 1 tsp. coriander
- 1 can (14 oz.) chopped tomatoes
- 2 large sweet potatoes, chopped into chunks
- Salt and pepper, to taste
- Large handful cilantro, roughly chopped

Method:
1. Preheat to oven to 356 degrees Fahrenheit.
2. Drizzle some olive oil into a large pot and place over a medium heat.
3. Place the onions into the pot and sauté until soft.
4. Add the minced beef and sauté until browned.
5. Add the black beans, chili powder, coriander and canned tomatoes, stir to combine.
6. Leave to simmer for about 10 minutes as you prepare the sweet potatoes.
7. Prick the sweet potatoes all over and place into the microwave, cook on HIGH for 1 minute increments until soft all the way through.

8. Cut the sweet potatoes into chunks and place into a bowl, mash with a potato masher or fork, add a pinch of salt and pepper and stir through.
9. Pour the mince and bean mixture into a large baking dish and spread the mashed sweet potatoes over top.
10. Sprinkle the coriander over the top of the sweet potatoes.
11. Place into the oven and bake for approximately 30 minutes until golden.
12. Leave to cool before cutting into 8 pieces, stacking into your airtight container/and store in the fridge or freezer until needed.

Swiss Chard and Ricotta Crust-Less Pie

Swiss chard, ricotta, eggs and a little bit of grated cheddar are the key ingredients in this protein-heavy, carb-light pie. Because there's no crust or pastry base, this is really more like a quiche, but "pie" always sounds better to me! Because it's very low in calories, you could serve it with a robust green salad with added nuts seeds, and perhaps some roasted root veggies. Ideal for dinners on nights where you don't want to, or shouldn't go for a full-on, heavy meal.

Serves: 6 slices

Container: you will need 1 large container or 6 small ones if storing or freezing individually. If storing in 1 large one, separate the slices with greaseproof paper so they don't stick together.

Time: approximately 30 minutes

Nutritional info per serving:

- Calories: 200
- Fat: 14 grams
- Protein: 14 grams
- Carbs: 4 grams

Ingredients:

- Butter or cooking oil spray
- 5 eggs
- 9 oz. ricotta cheese
- 4 cups shredded Swiss chard
- 1 onion, finely chopped
- ½ cup grated cheddar cheese
- Handful of fresh parsley, finely chopped
- ½tsp baking powder
- Salt and pepper, to taste

Method:

1. Preheat the oven to 356 degrees Fahrenheit and grease a baking dish with butter or cooking oil spray.
2. Place all ingredients, plus a pinch of salt and pepper into a bowl and whisk until fully combined.

3. Pour into your prepared baking dish and place into the oven.
4. Bake for approximately 25 minutes or until just set and beginning to turn golden on top.
5. Slice into 6 pieces, pack into your chosen containers cover and store in the fridge or freezer until needed!
6. A small drop of tomato relish goes really well on the side of this crust-less pie.

Steak and Zoodle Salad

"Zoodles" are noodles made from zucchinis. They've become rather popular over the last few years, as they have barely any calories but still resemble the look, texture and flavor-carrying abilities of noodles. Strips of steak, sprinkles of sesame seeds, and a lemony-olive oil dressing. Ideal for both dinner and lunch!

Serves: 4
Container: you will need 4 airtight containers, or 1 large container
Time: approximately 25 minutes

Nutritional info per serving:
- Calories: 365
- Fat: 22 grams
- Protein: 36 grams
- Carbs: 7 grams

Ingredients:
- 3 large zucchinis, cut into noodles with a spiralizer
- Saltand pepper, to taste
- Olive oil
- 2 sirloin steaks (or 1 really large one, use your judgment to figure out how much steak you'd like for each serving)
- Juice of one lemon mixed with 2 tbsp. olive oil
- 2 tbsp. sesame seeds

Method:
1. Place the zucchini noodles into a microwave-safe bowl and cook in the microwave for 1 minute. Don't overcook them, as you don't want them to be slushy or mushy! Sprinkle with salt and pepper and set aside.
2. Heat a small amount of olive oil in a non-stick frying pan and place over a high heat.
3. Place your steak onto the hot frying pan and cook to your liking, place onto a board to rest. You can season the steak with salt and pepper at this stage.
4. Keep the pan on the heat and add the sesame seeds to the pan and toast them in the leftover steak juices until golden and fragrant.
5. Thinly slice your steak and add to the bowl of zoodles, add the sesame seeds and the olive oil and lemon dressing, stir to combine.
6. Pack away into your container/s, cover and place into the fridge to store until needed!
7. I love to eat this salad cold, right out of the fridge.

Stir-Fried Brown Rice with Chicken and Veggie Jewels

I call the veggies in this dish "jewels" because they are cut into little squares and their glossy red, green and orange colors shine amongst the earthy brown rice and chicken. And sometimes, it's just more fun to name a dish with romantic words!

Serves: 4
Container: you will need 4 airtight containers
Time: approximately 35 minutes

Nutritional info per serving:
- Calories: 420
- Fat: 12 grams
- Protein: 21 grams
- Carbs: 61 grams

Ingredients:
- 2 large chicken breasts
- Olive oil
- Salt and pepper
- 1 tsp. chili flakes
- 1 ½ cups dry brown rice
- 1 garlic clove, crushed
- 2 red bell peppers, core and seeds removed, cut into small pieces
- 2 scallions, finely chopped
- 8 spears of asparagus, cut into small pieces (the same size as the bell pepper pieces)
- 2 carrots, peeled and cut into pieces to match the asparagus and bell pepper pieces
- 2 tbsp. olive oil mixed with 1 tbsp. soy sauce

Method:
1. Preheat the oven to 356 degrees Fahrenheit and line a baking tray with baking paper.
2. Place the chicken breasts on the tray and drizzle with olive oil, salt, pepper and chili flakes, place into the oven for approximately 20 minutes or until the chicken is cooked through.
3. Leave the chicken to rest for a few minutes before cutting into small pieces.

4. Cook the rice while the chicken is cooking: place the brown rice into a pot and add 2 cups of water, place over a high heat and bring to the boil, reduce to a simmer and cook with the lid on until the water has disappeared and the rice is cooked.

5. Add the garlic, peppers, scallions, asparagus and carrot to the pot of rice and add the olive oil and soy sauce mixture, turn the heat up to high and keep stirring as the veggies cook in the rice – you can use a wok or fry pan for this step, but I just use the pot the rice cooked in to save myself another dish to wash up! It works perfectly well.

6. Add the chopped cooked chicken to the pot, stir through and leave to cool before dishing into your containers, cover and store in the fridge or freezer until needed!

Prepped Quinoa Sushi Rolls

Quinoa is a healthy substitute for regular sushi rice. These sushi rolls don't contain any meat, so they are fine to be left in the fridge for a few days and feasted on as a light dinner. Tofu, veggies, quinoa, nori and sesame seeds – fresh and tasty!

Serves: 6 sushi rolls (about 1 roll per serving)
Container: you will need 1 large container
Time: approximately 25 minutes

Nutritional info per serving:
- Calories: 280
- Fat: 9 grams
- Protein: 18 grams
- Carbs: 29 grams

Ingredients:
- 1 cup quinoa
- 1 ½ cups water
- 14 oz. firm tofu, cut into strips
- 2 tbsp. soy sauce
- 1 tsp. sesame oil
- 1 tbsp. honey
- 6 nori sheets (sushi seaweed)
- 2 tbsp. sesame seeds, lightly toasted in a dry fry pan
- 1 red bell pepper, core and seeds removed, sliced
- 1 carrot, peeled and sliced into thin strips

Method:
1. Thoroughly rinse the quinoa in a sieve to remove the bitter outer layer.
2. Bring the water to the boil in a small pot and add the quinoa, stir to combine then turn the heat down to a simmer, cover, and cook for 12-15 minutes or until the liquid has disappeared and the quinoa is soft.
3. While the quinoa is cooking, prepare the tofu: place the soy sauce, sesame oil, honey and tofu into a small fry pan over a medium heat, cook for a few minutes until golden and cooked through, set aside.
4. Lay the nori sheets onto a large board, have your tofu, cooked quinoa, toasted sesame seeds and sliced veggies close by.

5. Spread a thin layer of quinoa onto each nori sheet, leaving an inch-wide gap at the top of each sheet.
6. Lay the tofu, carrot and bell peppers in a line in the center of the nori sheet (horizontally).
7. Sprinkle the sesame seeds on top of the tofu and veggies on each nori sheet.
8. Tightly roll the sushi and seal the ends with warm water.
9. Don't slice yet, wait until you're ready to eat to slice just before eating.
10. Pack the sushi rolls into your container and store in the fridge until needed!

Breaded Fish for the Freezer

Tender white fish, coated in beaten egg and crispy bread crumbs. Pop into the freezer and pull out whenever you want a tasty and highly-nutritious dinner! Serve with boiled potatoes and peas for a classic, British-inspired supper, or put in a taco or burger for a comfort food twist.

Serves: 12 breaded fish pieces (from 4 fillets, I would say 6 servings in total)
Container: you will need a small airtight container with greaseproof paper to separate the layers of fish so they don't stick together in the freezer.
Time: approximately 15 minutes

Nutritional info per serving:

- Calories: 190
- Fat: 5 grams
- Protein: 25 grams
- Carbs: 17 grams

Ingredients:

- 2 eggs, lightly beaten
- 1 cup breadcrumbs mixed with a pinch of salt and pepper
- 4 large white fish filets, cut into 3 pieces each

Method:

1. Prepare by setting the working space with your beaten egg in a small bowl, and your breadcrumbs mixed with salt and pepper spread onto a plate, have your fish pieces next to them on a plate, ready to be dipped.
2. Have a tray lined with baking paper ready too, so you can put the coated fish on it to freeze.
3. Dip the fish pieces into the beaten eggs and transfer them straight into the breadcrumbs, turning to coat thoroughly on all sides.
4. Place the coated fish onto your lined tray, cover with plastic wrap and place into the freezer until almost frozen.
5. Place the almost-frozen fish pieces into your small container lined with baking paper, place another layer of paper between each layer of fish so they don't stick together.
6. Place straight into the oven from the freezer when you want to eat them! Don't thaw them out first.

Green Bean, Potato, and Pea Curry

If you skip the rice, this curry is actually very light, despite the decent dose of potatoes! Green beans, peas and coconut milk infused with quality store-bought green curry paste. Garnish with cilantro and red chili for a special and satisfying meal. This curry is fantastic for the freezer.

Serves: 6
Container: you will need 6 airtight containers
Time: approximately 30 minutes

Nutritional info per serving:
- Calories: 460
- Fat: 26 grams
- Protein: 11 grams
- Carbs: 47 grams

Ingredients:
- Olive oil
- 4 garlic cloves, finely chopped
- 1 onion, finely chopped
- 4 tbsp. store-bought green curry paste
- 5 large potatoes, cut into cubes or chunks
- 2 cups frozen green beans
- 2 cups frozen peas
- 1 cup (8fl oz.) chicken or vegetable broth
- 3 cups (24fl oz.) coconut milk
- Salt, to taste

Method:
1. Drizzle some olive oil into a large pot or pan and place over a medium heat.
2. Add the garlic, onions and curry paste, stir to combine and leave to sauté for a couple of minutes until the curry paste is fragrant.
3. Add the potatoes, beans, peas, broth and coconut milk to the pot and stir to combine, add a pinch of salt to season.
4. Allow the curry to boil for approximately 20 minutes or until the potatoes are soft but not mushy.
5. Leave to cool before dividing between your 6 containers, covering and placing into the fridge or freezer.

Coconut-Poached Fish with Peanuts and Asian Greens

White fish, lightly poached in coconut milk, sprinkled with peanuts and served on a bed of steamed bok choy. This dish might sound complex, but it's really so simple and wholesome. For some extra energy, serve with brown rice.

Serves: 4
Container: you will need 4 airtight containers
Time: approximately 25 minutes

Nutritional info per serving:
- Calories: 440
- Fat: 32 grams
- Protein: 42 grams
- Carbs: 10 grams

Ingredients:
- 1 ½ cups (12fl oz.) coconut milk
- 1 tsp. soy sauce
- 1 tsp. fish sauce
- 1 tsp. chili flakes
- 4 white fish filets
- 2 bunches of bok choi, base removed, leaves washed
- ½ cup roasted, salted peanuts
- 1 tsp. sesame oil

Method:
1. Add the coconut milk, soy sauce, fish sauce, chili flakes and fish filets into a deep fry pan or pot and place over a medium heat.
2. Bring to a gentle boil and leave to simmer for about 10 minutes or until the fish is just cooked.
3. Add the bok choi to the pot and place the lid onto the pot, leave for 1 minute to gently steam the bok choi.
4. Divide the fish, bok choi, and coconut milk between your 4 containers and sprinkle the peanuts and sesame oil over the top, cover and place into the fridge or freezer to store until needed.
5. If you like, a sprinkle of fresh chili and cilantro is a gorgeous addition before eating.

Taco Freezer Packets

These packets are just like the smoothie packets back in the Breakfast section, but they are for tacos! Chicken, bell peppers, onion, spices, and tomatoes all packed into sealable bags and stashed in the freezer. Simply leave them out to thaw then throw the contents into a hot fry pan to cook, then load onto a tortilla, add some guac and you're good to go!

Serves: 8 packets (1 packet per serving)
Container: you will need 8 freezer-friendly, sealable bags
Time: approximately 15 minutes

Nutritional info per serving:
- Calories: 170
- Fat: 5 grams
- Protein: 20 grams
- Carbs: 12 grams

Ingredients:
- 3 large chicken breasts, cut into small slices
- 3 red bell peppers, core and seeds removed, thinly sliced
- 2 red onions, red onions, thinly sliced
- 2 cans (14 oz.) chopped tomatoes
- 6 garlic cloves, finely chopped
- 2 tsp. paprika
- 1 tsp. ground cumin
- 1 tsp. ground coriander
- 1 tsp. chili powder
- 2 tbsp. olive oil

Method:
1. Place all ingredients into a large bowl and stir to combine, making sure every piece of chicken and vegetables is coated in olive oil and spices.
2. Divide the mixture between your 8 freezer-safe sealable bags, seal and stack into the fridge to store until needed.
3. Leave to thaw before sautéing in a hot frying pan until cooked all the way through and the onions and bell peppers are slightly charred.

Breaded Chicken Freezer Packets

This freezer packet features breaded chicken, which you can place on a baking tray and bake in the oven, straight from the freezer. Great for chicken and veggie tray bakes with any veggies you like! You'll thank yourself for prepping these protein-filled packets!

Serves: 8 freezer packets, each with 3 small pieces of chicken (1 serving per packet)
Container: you will need 8 freezer-friendly, sealable bags
Time: approximately 15 minutes

Nutritional info per serving:
- Calories: 265
- Fat: 3 grams
- Protein: 35 grams
- Carbs: 22 grams

Ingredients:
- 2 eggs, lightly beaten
- 2 cups breadcrumbs mixed with a pinch of salt and pepper
- 4 large chicken breasts, each cut into 6 pieces

Method:
1. Prepare your work space by placing the beaten egg in a small bowl next to a plate of breadcrumbs, salt and pepper.
2. Line a baking tray with baking paper and keep nearby so you can place your breaded chicken onto it.
3. Take your chicken pieces and dip them into the egg, then straight into the breadcrumbs, turning a few times to thoroughly coat in breadcrumbs.
4. Place the breaded chicken pieces onto your lined tray and place in the freezer.
5. Once frozen, divide the chicken pieces between your 8 freezer bags and stack into the freezer to store until needed!
6. To cook, simply preheat your oven to 356 degrees Fahrenheit, place the chicken pieces onto a lined baking tray and bake for about 25 minutes or until cooked through, no need to thaw first.

Marinated Steak Freezer Packets

Next in the freezer packet series is marinated steak. Tender strips of beef with a tasty marinade – perfect for stir-frying with veggies and serving on a little bed of brown rice!

Serves: 8 packets (1 serving per packet)
Container: you will need 8 freezer-friendly, sealable bags
Time: approximately 15 minutes

Nutritional info per serving:
- Calories: 220
- Fat: 10 grams
- Protein: 28 grams
- Carbs: 2 grams

Ingredients:
- 4 beef steaks, cut into slices
- 2 tbsp. olive oil
- 2 tbsp. soy sauce
- 1 tbsp. honey
- Salt and pepper, to taste

Method:
1. Place the steak strips, olive oil, soy sauce, honey, and a pinch of salt and pepper into a bowl and stir to combine, making sure each piece of beef is coated in oil, honey and sauce.
2. Divide the marinated steak between your 8 freezer-safe, sealable bags and stack into the freezer to store until needed.
3. To cook, leave to thaw in the bag before emptying into a hot frying pan to sauté with veggies, rice, egg or whatever you fancy!

Marinated Pork Packets

Slices of pork, marinated with simple herbs, olive oil and lemon juice. You can serve this pork with a side of fresh veggies and roasted potatoes, or in a pita bread with salad and Greek yoghurt.

Serves: 8 packets, (1 serving per packet)
Container: you will need 8 freezer-friendly, sealable bags
Time: approximately 15 minutes

Nutritional info per serving:
- Calories: 220
- Fat: 39 grams
- Protein: 21 grams
- Carbs: 2 grams

Ingredients:
- 4 pork steaks, cut into slices
- 2 tbsp. olive oil
- Juice of 1 lemon
- 1 small sprig of fresh rosemary, roughly chopped
- 1 tsp. dried mixed herbs (use fresh herbs if you have them, but don't worry if you don't, dried herbs are fine)
- 4 garlic cloves, crushed

Method:
1. Place all ingredients into a bowl and stir to combine, making sure the pork is thoroughly coated in oil, lemon juice, garlic and herbs.
2. Divide between your 8 freezer-safe bags, seal and stack into the freezer to store until needed.
3. Leave to thaw before cooking in a hot frying pan.

Prepped Pasta Sauce: Tomato

Keeping frozen pasta sauces in the freezer is one of the best ways to utilize the magic of meal prepping. Boil some wholegrain or gluten free pasta and throw one of these sauce packets into a pot to thaw and cook through. The first one in this series is a simple and tasty tomato sauce.

Serves: 4 containers of sauce (each container has enough sauce for 3 servings of pasta)
Container: you will need 4 airtight, freezer-friendly containers
Time: approximately 25 minutes

Nutritional info per serving:
- Calories: 55
- Fat: 3 grams
- Protein: 1 gram
- Carbs: 8 grams

Ingredients:
- Olive oil
- 6 garlic cloves, finely chopped
- 2 onions, finely chopped
- 3 cans (14 oz.) chopped tomatoes
- 2 tbsp. balsamic vinegar
- 1 tsp. honey
- 1 tsp. mixed dried herbs
- Salt and pepper, to taste

Method:
1. Drizzle the olive oil into a frying pan and place over a medium heat.
2. Add the garlic and onions to the pan and sauté until soft.
3. Add the tomatoes, balsamic vinegar, honey, herbs, and a pinch of salt and pepper, stir to combine.
4. Cover the pot and leave to simmer on a low heat for 20 minutes.
5. Leave the sauce to cool slightly before dividing between your 4 containers, cover, and pack into the freezer to store until needed!
6. You could also use this sauce for zucchini noodles and meatballs!

Prepped Pasta Sauce: Pesto

This sauce is not for the freezer, but for the fridge. Spoon it into a glass jar or airtight container and place a dollop onto your zoodles or wholegrain pasta next time you're in a rush for dinner. You don't need much of this pesto, as it has a strong and rich flavor. Ideal for people who have lots of basil growing in their herb garden!

Serves: makes enough for about 12 servings of pasta or zoodles
Container: you will need 1 glass jar with a lid, or a sealable container
Time: approximately 10 minutes

Nutritional info per serving:
- Calories: 130
- Fat: 12 grams
- Protein: 4 grams
- Carbs: 1 gram

Ingredients:
- 2 cups fresh basil leaves
- 3.5 oz. parmesan cheese, broken into small chunks
- 1/3 cup olive oil
- 3 garlic cloves, roughly chopped
- ½ cup pine nuts, (they are very expensive so just use cashew nuts for a cheaper option!)
- Salt and pepper, to taste

Method:
1. Place all ingredients into a blender or small food processor and add a pinch of salt and pepper.
2. Blend until smooth but still with a few small pieces of nuts remaining.
3. Pour into your jar or container and store in the fridge until needed!
4. You can also use this as a salad dressing for potato salads or chicken salads.

Prepped Pasta Sauce: Creamy Mushroom

This creamy sauce uses part sour cream and part yoghurt for a tangy and slightly lighter option. This earthy mushroom sauce is lovely on pasta or zoodles, but it's also ideal when served on grilled steak or chicken. Keep a few packets of this sauce in the freezer and throw straight into a pot over a medium heat when you want to use it!

Serves: 4 containers of sauce (each container has enough for about 3 servings)
Container: you will need 4 airtight, freezer-safe containers
Time: approximately 20 minutes

Nutritional info per serving:
- Calories: 80
- Fat: 4 grams
- Protein: 2 grams
- Carbs: 3 grams

Ingredients:
- 2 tbsp. olive oil
- 5 cups chopped mushrooms, (use a range of different kinds of mushrooms if you like! I use white button mushrooms and Portobello mushrooms)
- 8 garlic cloves, finely chopped
- 1 sprig of fresh rosemary, finely chopped
- 3fl oz. white wine
- ½ cup (4fl oz.) sour cream
- ½ cup (4fl oz.) plain yogurt

Method:
1. Drizzle the olive oil into a frying pan and place over a medium heat.
2. Add the mushrooms, garlic and rosemary or mixed herbs, sauté for a few minutes until the mushrooms have begun to shrink and become colored.
3. Add the wine and simmer until the alcohol evaporates.
4. Add the sour cream and yoghurt and stir to combine.
5. Turn off the heat and leave the sauce to cool slightly before dividing into your 4 containers, cover and place into the freezer to store until needed!

Healthy Lamb Curry with Couscous

Couscous is a tasty alternative to rice, and it goes so well with this tasty lamb curry. Tomatoes, spices, onions and lamb cook together to create a rich and aromatic curry to soak into a small bed of soft couscous. Great for the freezer!

Serves: 6
Container: you will need 6 airtight containers
Time: approximately 30 minutes

Nutritional info per serving:
- Calories: 650
- Fat: 29 grams
- Protein: 43 grams
- Carbs: 52 grams

Ingredients:
- Olive oil
- 2 onions roughly chopped
- 1 tsp. ground turmeric
- 1 tsp. chili powder
- 1 tsp. dried cumin
- 1 tsp. dried coriander
- ½ tsp. cinnamon
- 20 oz. lamb steak (leg steak works great), cut into cubes
- 2 cups (16fl oz.) lamb stock
- 2 cans (14 oz.) chopped tomatoes
- Salt and pepper, to taste
- 2 cups dried couscous

Method:
1. Drizzle some olive oil into a large frying pan or pot and place over a medium heat.
2. Add the onions, turmeric, chili powder, cumin, coriander and cinnamon and heat until the onions are soft.
3. Add the lamb cubes and stir to coat in spices and onions, sauté for a couple of minutes to brown the meat.
4. Add the lamb stock, tomatoes, salt and pepper, stir to combine.

5. Place the lid onto the pot or pan and allow it to simmer over a low heat for about 25 minutes until the lamb is cooked and the curry sauce is rich and beginning to thicken.
6. While the curry cooks, prepare the couscous: place the dried couscous into a bowl and pour 2 and a half cups of boiling water over, cover the bowl and leave for about 5 minutes until the couscous is soft.
7. Uncover the couscous and add a pinch of salt and pepper, use a fork to fluff the couscous and then divide it between your 6 containers.
8. Divide the lamb curry between the containers and spoon it on top of the couscous, cover and place into the fridge or freezer to store until needed!

Salmon with Mango and Lentils

Treat yourself to a salmon dinner and make it a special one with mango and lentils. You can easily freeze this dish as salmon is preserved really well in the freezer. I like to make this dish when I feel like my body is calling out for healthy fats and some major fiber!

Serves: 4
Container: you will need 4 airtight containers
Time: approximately 20 minutes

Nutritional info per serving:
Calories: 315
Fat: 9 grams
Protein: 30 grams
Carbs: 26 grams

Ingredients:
- Olive oil
- 2 large salmon steaks, cut in half to make 4 even pieces
- 1 tbsp. soy sauce
- 1 tsp. sweet chili sauce
- 2 cups cooked brown lentils (I used canned ones, so much easier!)
- 1 ripe mango, skin removed, flesh cut into small chunks
- 4 fresh mint leaves, finely chopped

Method:
1. Drizzle some olive oil into a non-stick fry pan and place over a medium heat.
2. Add the salmon pieces to the hot pan skin-side down and cook for 2 minutes on each side or until just cooked through.
3. Pour the soy sauce and chili sauce over the salmon.
4. Divide the lentils between your 4 containers, add the mango to each container, then place a piece of salmon on top, finish by sprinkling each pieces of salmon with the fresh mint.
5. Cover the containers and place into the fridge or freezer until needed!

Freezer Chicken Soup

This soup is an extremely light meal, filled with minerals and nutrients to restore you after a binge-full weekend. Chicken, broth, corn and scallions come together to melt into a tasty and wholesome soup to make you feel nourished.

Serves: 6
Container: you will need 6 freezer-safe, airtight containers
Time: approximately 30 minutes

Nutritional info per serving:
- Calories: 230
- Fat: 9 grams
- Protein: 25 grams
- Carbs: 12 grams

Ingredients:
- 5 boneless chicken thighs, cut into small pieces
- 1 onion, finely chopped
- 4 cups (32fl oz.) chicken broth
- 2 cups (16fl oz.) water
- 1 can (14 oz.) corn kernels, drained
- 2 scallions, finely sliced
- Salt and pepper, to taste

Method:
1. Place all ingredients into a pot and add a pinch of salt and pepper, place over a medium heat and cover.
2. Leave to simmer for approximately 30 minutes until the chicken is cooked through.
3. Leave to cool slightly before dividing into your 6 containers, cover and stack into the freezer to store until needed.
4. Leave the frozen containers on the bench to thaw before thoroughly reheating, or simply place the frozen soup in a pot over a high heat to speed the process up!

Conclusion

Once you get the hang of meal prepping you will never want to go back! Having packets of fresh, healthy food packed away in the fridge and freezer, ready to be eaten is a satisfying and gratifying feeling. If these recipes do not quite fit in with your particular weight-loss diet, then simply modify them until the macronutrients are where you want them to be! Less carbs? No worries. More protein? Easy. Just download a calorie-counting app, load the recipes in, and shuffle things around to reach your desired numbers.

Always remember to prep meals that you *want to eat!* In my opinion, the best foods are healthy *and* delicious, and once you hit that sweet-spot you can lose weight without even noticing that you've changed your diet! You'll be so satisfied and full from your yummy, nutrient-filled foods that you won't get that horrible sense of deprivation and craving which comes with many strict diets.

Make a day of it and go shopping for containers, oils, spices, non-perishables, masking tape and sharpies for labeling, a diary to plan your meals and prep days, and put it all in a pretty and space-saving box.

Make your prep-sessions fun and relaxing, as they should be! You deserve to enjoy your life, your diet, and your kitchen.

Good luck and have fun!

Made in the USA
Middletown, DE
15 February 2018